Shameless Propositions

Shameless Propositions

Women's Sexuality and Theoretical Authority

Alice Adams

Madison • Teaneck
Fairleigh Dickinson University Press

Associated University Presses
2010 Eastpark Boulevard
Cranbury, NJ 08512

The paper used in this publication meets the requirements of the American National Standard for Permanence of Paper for Printed Library Materials
Z39.48–1984.

Library of Congress Cataloging-in-Publication Data

Adams, Alice E. (Alice Elaine), 1957-
Shameless propostions : women's sexuality and theoretical authority / Alice Adams.
p. cm.
Includes bibliographical references and index.
ISBN 978-0-8386-4259-7 (alk. paper)
1. Women—Sexuality behavior. I. Title.
HQ29.A33 2010
306.7082—dc22

2009031297

PRINTED IN THE UNITED STATES OF AMERICA

For Liz,
Agent Provocateuse

Contents

Shameless Propositions

Introduction

Shameless Propositions is about how scientific ideas about sexuality, especially women's sexuality, achieve authority. This is of necessity a skeptic's project. Scientific inquiry into sexuality, in common with scientific investigations of similarly charged questions about racial difference or the existence of God, is particularly vulnerable to the influence of our desires, anxieties, half- or unexamined assumptions, personal agendas, and moral prescriptions. For anyone who wants the truth of sexuality, therefore, the most welcome critiques are those that attempt to remove all that is prejudicial. From whatever facts remain when the subjective excrescences are scraped away, one could hope to construct an accurate model of what it is like to be sexed, gendered, and sexual.

As it turns out, that is very hard to do. Establishing a position of scientific authority in relation to sexuality is dependent less on one's command of the facts than on one's ability to negotiate the fears, territorialism, questionable precedents, and expectations that one's conclusions be applicable to moral questions. It occurred to me during my initial research for *Shameless Propositions* that it might not be possible to get past the extra stuff and arrive at a clean understanding. Only later did it dawn on me that there was no extra stuff, and that even the bad ideas are integral to sexuality as we know it. By "bad ideas" I mean those that relate loosely to the evidence produced to support them as well as those that have energized damaging stereotypes. The bad ideas and all the sincere attempts to deconstruct those ideas—both are more essential to how we live our sexuality than any empirical data.

The rest of this introduction is an explanation of this guiding idea, and the remainder of the book explores how it happens that sexuality emerges from tensions between our biological and social capacities, between what we do and how we interpret what we do. For me this required the sacrifice of what seems now a naive hope that it would be possible to see beyond the thorny overgrowth that is the history, science, and politics of sexuality. The truth is that what appear to be obstacles to real knowledge are essential components of the object under study. They can be renegotiated, and strong resistance can open up some clear ground, but they cannot be done away with.

It is as if we are universally shortsighted and in need of correction, and so none of us enjoys an unmediated encounter with the facts. We do, however, have some choice about what corrective lens to use. What anyone in search of the facts would like to remove—the interpretive and therefore distorting lens—is what makes it possible to know sexuality at all. Those who achieve authority are the mediators; their ideas, their interpretations, grind the lenses through which we see sexuality.

This metaphor is in its own way shortsighted, however, because the kind of sexuality I am addressing is not a separate, stationary object on the other side of a lens. The whole scene moves together as an inseparable whole. Sexual human beings, the authoritative experts, and the ideas they generate about sexuality have to be considered as one in order to understand not just isolated biological or social aspects of sexuality, but what sexuality really is. Taken together, the scientific, religious, literary, political, and popular discourses that refer to sexuality—all of them heavily encrusted with the messy debris of human passion—are sexuality.

The basic postmodern insight that one cannot peel reality from its representations is easy to misinterpret as an argument that nothing exists beneath the brittle shell of our perception. Wherever a crack materializes, and there are plenty of those in the discourses on sexuality, it reveals not some valuable, previously unimagined bit of our reality, but just an empty space in urgent need of a patch. The holes are plainly marked. They occur wherever one encounters disputed, confusing, absent, or illogical findings. Anyone with a serious interest in the discourses on sexuality will feel the pull to enter the dispute, expose the illogic, and resolve the confusion; in other words; to craft a reality sufficient to cover over the exposed emptiness.

One of the deepest holes is the dispute about whether, and in what way, heterosexuality is better than homosexuality. Joining this dispute means taking a position about whether heterosexuality exists as a distinct sexual orientation and identity. Of the currently available positions, two are most authoritative. One argues that heterosexuality is indeed a discrete orientation, a sexual and social identity quite distinct from homosexuality. The other says that dividing people according to sexual orientation is a foolish and misleading project. Both positions enable value judgments based on sexual orientation: perhaps what distinguishes heterosexuality from homosexuality are also the attributes that make it superior, or perhaps there is no need to divide people by sexual orientation because everyone is essentially heterosexual, although some go sadly off course.

The most influential arguments for the superiority or totality of heterosexuality cite reproductive interests, God's law, nature, and the preferences of the majority. To illustrate what it means to understanding the reality of sexuality as a matter of gaps, biases, and passions, I will turn to what one could be forgiven for thinking was a dead argument for the primacy of heterosexuality, one that centered on the proposition that there was a physiological and psychological difference between vaginal and clitoral orgasms. Masters and Johnson (1966) established as authoritative the conclusion that trying to define a difference was fruitless. But the vaginal orgasm, never fully abandoned, lives on most prominently on in certain genital surgeries and the continuing search for an obscure "G" spot, a site of clitoris-like sensitivity in the interior of the vagina.

One of the latest contributions to this debate was made by psychologist Stuart Brody (2006). Brody, taking exception to the argument that "all sexual behaviours are equal," maintained that heterosexual sex is not only psychologically superior, but physiologically as well (393). The only sexual behavior that can actually improve our health and well-being is "penile-vaginal intercourse," performed without hand-to-clitoris or other intrusions. For women in particular, Brody claims, the vaginal orgasms that result from pure intercourse are measurably better, and make women feel happier, than clitoral orgasms.

At first reading, Brody's rehashing of these old ideas might seem hardly worth noticing. However, he has published rather prolifically and at least in Britain has achieved national attention. This renders ironic his complaint that he is being censored by the academic left, but it is nonetheless an effective rhetorical strategy, drawing attention away from his claims and inviting the reader to focus instead on the maker of those claims. Brody (2007) compares himself to a martyred artist: "I am unable to play the piano, but it doesn't mean I don't appreciate Vladimir Horowitz," he says. "I don't say that he doesn't exist and I don't try to break his fingers" (quoted in Bowditch).

Whatever else it might indicate, this pileup of desperate rhetoric—portraying himself as a maestro of sexology and translating academic opposition into the denial of his authority, a violation of his right of free speech, and a physical and existential assault—signal that Brody is trying at one and the same time to cover some holes in the story about the revelation of heterosexuality's transcendence and to establish his own authority to make that repair.

Looking at the relative success of someone like Brody reveals a great deal about how we constitute our sexuality—at least as much, I believe, as focusing on the work of more credible experts. Success in this sense does not mean settling the question; it means perpetuating it. One can succeed at this very well without ever furnishing compelling evidence in support of one's argument. Brody succeeds by using his research to reinforce his own reason for being: there would be no need to defend heterosexuality, and hence no need for a defender like Brody, unless the heterosexual dominance was being undermined by tolerance for alternative sexual behaviors and identities.

What does all this have to do with determining the reality of human sexuality? Assuming it could be answered satisfactorily, the question of whether orgasms induced by straight intercourse might be somehow superior to other orgasms would tell us much less about what it means to be sexual than does the fact that the question attracts so much attention. Brody has set up shop at one of the biggest fissures in our sexuality—exactly where debates about the moral value of various sexualities have yet to be settled—and is trying to be the one who finally plugs the hole. By claiming to have produced proof of the physiological superiority of a heterosexually induced orgasm, Brody injects a bit of new life into old claims about the moral superiority of heterosexuality.

Even if he were promoting an idea I considered worthwhile, I would not care for Brody's rhetoric, in particular that he bases his claim to authoritative expertise on the premise that everyone else is not only wrong but repressive. But no matter what I, or the sexologists he casts as censors of truth, think of ideas like Brody's, the fact is that sexuality as we know it is so replete with myth, political maneuvering, reaching for elusive proofs, and imperfectly disguised bias that if all that were excised we wouldn't be able to recognize what remained as sexuality.

What counts as reality is whatever affirms one's sense of worth, belonging, humanity, even being itself. Revelations like Masters and Johnson's, that a previously authoritative story about sexuality rests on a shaky theoretical foundation, will be welcomed by those who are as a result relieved of guilt or shame. But to others any attempt to challenge a general truth—

here, that heterosexuality is superior to any other orientation—will represent a threat just as deeply personal. As Kinsey and Masters and Johnson showed, what is generally said and believed about sexuality often doesn't align with how people actually live their sexual lives, but that doesn't mean that the missions like Brody's are irrelevant. There is nothing trivial about the ways that we use words to construct and deconstruct our truths.

It is not possible to think or act as a sexual person without implicating oneself in the major discourses on sexuality and answering to propositions about the relative value of sexual behaviors and identities. This premise can be tested by trying to imagine what it would be like to live in a world where all the major discourses on sexuality—religious, scientific, popular, and political—went silent about the question of what causes homosexuality, and where questions about whether it is right or wrong, permissible or forbidden, would produce a universal shrug. What makes that utopia so nearly unthinkable is also what makes the major discourses on sexuality effective: they keep alive the quest for the truth about the difference between men and women, heterosexual and homosexual, normal and perverse.

It is this sexuality, the one that appears in public as an authoritative spokesman for the expertise of psychologists, endocrinologists, politicians, religious leaders and other specialists, the one that points to us—human beings, that is—as objects of analysis, that I am interested in examining in *Shameless Propositions.* This public sexuality is, in postmodern fashion, the sum total of how it is seen and what has been claimed about it, but its surface is also the door to insubordinate questions about who is responsible, who benefits, and who loses as the stories and the arguments circulate.

Feminist colleagues have sometimes challenged me to construct models of women's sexuality more potently true than those the conventional discourses have produced. In effect, I have been asked to furnish a generally intelligible story about women's sexuality that unlike the conventional versions corresponds to the reality of women's lives. My fullest answer to that challenge is in chapter 4, but in short, I couldn't even make the attempt without remaking myself in the image of experts like Brody, and I lack the will to do that. It wasn't that the professional experts, or the writers of trendy articles for women's magazines, or the everyday woman in the street got the taxonomies and the developmental stories wrong; it was that my ideas about what it meant to be correct had to change.

Whenever the experts reveal some new fact about women's sexuality (about our orgasmic capacities, the influence of our hormones or mothers, the incidence of homosexuality among us, how often we think about sex, etc., almost into infinity), its fate is determined in large part by how comprehensible it is in relation to already accepted ideas. If it fits, it may, like the vaginal orgasm, live on for decades after critics and common sense have discredited it.

And yet someday, at least according to a more confident story about the power of science, our understanding will advance so far that questions like "how (and why?) do women have orgasms?" will have been finally resolved. Speaking not about orgasm but about the biology of sexual orientation, neuroanatomist Simon LeVay (1993) represents this kind of optimism, writing that we will "have the human species in a bottle, dissected, labeled, catalogued and explained in all its delightful and repellent diversity" (29).

The comprehensive revelations LeVay anticipates are part of a scientific fiction as compelling as the story of the vaginal orgasm. A scientific fiction is an imaginative interpretation of what happens when science encounters natural phenomena. The scientific fictions about women and orgasm discussed above are all enlivened by the same perception that motivates LeVay's metaphor. They all seek to present a plausible sequence of events that is at once the story of the natural phenomenon—female orgasm, sexual orientation—and the story of the scientist, methodically following every uncertainty to its ultimate resolution. Such fictions must be widely culturally intelligible to be effective, and the image LeVay employs—humanity in a bottle—helps make his fiction vivid enough to be appealing or dismaying, depending on what one hopes science can accomplish.

Being fictional does not mean that projections like LeVay's are necessarily false. They are instead somewhat like legal fictions: they make assertions that cannot be proven, but that make it possible to go forward. In law, such fictions facilitate judicial proceedings; in science, most obviously as the media delivers it and the public receives it, they can help build consensus or stimulate conflict. Scientific fictions oversimplify ideas, distort our understanding, and attempt to squeeze certainty from equivocal propositions, but for better or worse they are what make science meaningful.

Who tells the story matters. From the development of modern science in the seventeenth century, Donna Haraway (1997) excavated the concept of the modest witness. "Only those who could disappear 'modestly' could really witness with authority rather than gawk with curiosity" (25). The modest witness's biases were protected behind notions of "heroic action in science," which is to say, the power to uncover the hidden secrets of nature.

He was further protected by the exclusion of those who might see differently, who, marked by their color, sex, and class, could in Haraway's words be "evacuated of agency" and identified as objects of scientific observation (32). I have been acutely aware, particularly in my approach to psychology and endocrinology, that I am an outsider and, more than occasionally, their tacit object. The queer girl I introduce in the following section is also a teller of stories, though her (or rather my) fictions are obviously personal, made up of experience and partial insights. She is an avowedly constructed observer, at home—if not comfortable—amid the many relics that have passed as universally relevant truths in their own place and time.

Authority speaks

In one of my last papers as an undergraduate English major, I argued that Rochester's first wife in Charlotte Brontë's *Jane Eyre* (1848) was ensnared in the contradiction between colluding with and defying her husband's power over her. The resulting madness, I believed, held the whole narrative together. When Bertha died, her careening rage silenced, there was really nothing left to say. It seemed as if the second wife fared better than the first because she could speak for herself. She didn't have to plead in grunts to an uncomprehending audience. But her story ended at the point where she took the first wife's place, as if like Bertha she had surrendered her voice when she married. That the narrative produces in Bertha a racially stereotyped Other did not occur to me; that Jane might fear, as Susan Meyer (1989) put it, "becoming black" like her predecessor was an idea as unavailable to my mind as it was unspoken in the novel (151). But it had at least dawned on me that something unspoken could be the very thing compelling the story to continue.

My professor explained that the argument I made was marred by feminism. To underscore his assessment, he gave me the first B I had earned writing literary criticism. My thinking had diverged far enough from the authorized knowledge to be marginal.

Now I occupy a position akin to my professor's, and the questions about what counts as authorized knowledge are no less relevant for me and my students: How does authority, understood not as a foundation but as an effect of discourse, nevertheless determine who should be granted a voice and who should sit quiet?

A long education in the formulas of academia has not resolved these questions, but I have witnessed again and again the terms of the relation that first brought them into my consciousness. I read Virginia Woolf's critique of *Jane Eyre* as if she were my English professor, still looming over me. Woolf explained why the novel, which had elements of greatness, was "deformed and twisted" (1957, 72). She was particularly concerned with a scene in which Brontë put a bit of feminist polemic in Jane's mouth. Jane argues that women chafe at confinement and would prefer self-determination to knitting. Then she hears the chilling laughter from nowhere that will eventually lead to the discovery of Bertha, the deformed and twisted madwoman in the attic. The interruption of the narrative offended Woolf, who wrote that in the grip of anger, Brontë "left her story, to which her entire devotion was due, to attend to some personal grievance" (76).

For Woolf, Jane's divergence demonstrated Brontë's lack of artistic integrity. "What one means by integrity, in the case of the novelist, is the conviction that he gives one that this is the truth" (75). I do find Brontë convincing, but I am not looking for what Woolf sought. When Brontë has Jane say that it is thoughtless to condemn or laugh at women who want to do more than make puddings, she is speaking to no one except her assumed reader. What answers her is, in fact, disembodied laughter, as if that reader has responded with the jeering Jane feared.

Before confronting what she thought of as Brontë's failure, Woolf had been grappling with Professor von X, putative author of *The Mental, Moral, and Physical Inferiority of the Female Sex*. His exercise of authority angered her, but his influence seemed to be at work in her conviction that a woman writer is defective unless she can forget her sex (108). According to Woolf, if a woman writer remembers her sex, then her grievances against men, her rage, will rot her art. The dismissive reader that looms in Jane's "feminist statement" is very much like Woolf. Woolf wanted women, or at least women of her approximate class, race, and nation, to have the independent means Brontë's character lacked, but for Woolf money and opportunity were not enough to guarantee artistic integrity. That entity is the offspring of a heterosexual metaphor: "Some collaboration has to take place in the mind between the woman and man before the act of creation can be accomplished. Some marriage of opposites has to be consummated" (108).

This union of opposites is a fiction, but in common with the comparable scientific fictions I discussed earlier, that is not its offense. The offense is in the cultural work it does. Departing from the marriage plot Woolf advocated leads to the birth of a perverse third, configured in Woolf's imagination as a woman's fury, triviality, vulgarity and bestiality. If art is to survive, that alien, like Bertha in Brontë's novel, must be exiled to the domain of what is unthought and unspoken. When Brontë strayed, she excluded herself from the privileged circle of those novelists who manage to convince the reader that they are telling the truth.

I am compelled to deal with sexuality because it serves as the primary metaphoric foundation for anyone seeking to explain women's psychology, ethics, spirituality, artistic aspirations, and erotic lives. Most of the "fictions" about women's sexuality I will examine in the first part of *Shameless Propositions* are neither literary nor consciously political. Instead, they have been generated in psychology, medicine, and research science, areas of expertise in which authority is not supposed to be achieved by means of a great metaphor, but on the strength of observed facts milled by hard logic.

Nevertheless, throughout *Shameless Propositions* I am hunting for better fictions. They tend to turn up where one might expect, wherever there are holes in the narrative. In the second part of the book, that hunger sends me in search of experts unthought of in Woolf's day: female, queer, or feminist psychologists, scientists, and philosophers. In their appropriations and revisions of established thought, I have looked for some solutions to the predicament of those who, like Bertha, have traditionally figured as perverse, and who continue to function as the sign of what a disciplined mind excludes.

What we now refer to as sexuality is no more than what can show itself as performance, narrative, research subject, and social identity. Its proper mode is metaphorical. The queer, the feminist, the woman—these are constructions that stand for something else that cannot or must not show itself: silence, holes, lies, babbling, masks, and the morally unthinkable. Sexuality is itself a metaphor, distinguished by definition from the unspeakable, amorphous, inessential eroticism or rage for which it stands. Sexuality is the metaphor through which disciplinary experts seek to establish their authority, but their undisciplined objects of study have often proved more formidable, and more convincing, than any science dreamed of.

Voices Granted and Denied

I begin my search for better fictions by exploring the limits of those I've already broached, an endeavor uncomfortably akin to the attempt of the protagonist of *The Yellow Wallpaper* to scrape away at the layers of her confinement. Speaking for oneself from such an outsider's position means sacrificing a great deal of authority, if not sanity.

The madwoman and the pervert have something in common in that they both lack the authority to speak to their own condition and are liable to confinement. One of the early experts who defined the pervert's condition was Morton Prince, an eminent neurologist who was instrumental in developing modern concepts of abnormal psychology. Prince's views on the reliability of perverts' autobiographies have been dissected by Julian Carter (1997) and Siobhan Somerville (1994). Prince's essential argument was that perverts' autobiographies (and, by extension, case histories based on autobiographical material) were useless because any appearance of narrative coherence in a pervert's story was illusory: "Probably there is no class of people whose statements will less stand the test of a scorching cross-examination than the moral pervert. One cannot help feeling that if the pervert was thus examined by an independent observer, instead of being allowed to tell his own story without interruption, a different tale would be told, or great gaps would be found, which are now nicely bridged, or many asserted facts would be resolved into pure inferences" (p.92).

The ability to produce a coherent narrative—i.e., a story that covers its gaps effectively—is evidence of perversion in a perverse person. The shrewd scientific observer will interrupt the deception and insert in its place "a different tale," one suited to his own agenda. Prince's assertions about the special unreliability of perverts are only meaningful if one is ready to believe that science is truly independent, that it has no part in the production of the pervert, and that there is such a thing as an independent observer with the power to bottle us up—to return to LeVay's metaphor—in all our "delightful and repellant diversity."

But if the story science tells covers up the gaps that another story (say, that of the pervert or the madwoman) reveals, what differentiates it from the pervert's story?

Answering that means returning to the question of who tells the story. I will interrupt the story of Prince to return to Woolf, whose sense of irony compelled her to reveal what Prince had to conceal in order to maintain his authority. She remarked at the opening of *A Room of One's Own* that " 'I' is only a convenient term for somebody who has no real being. Lies will flow from my lips" (4). This "I" entered the British Museum claiming with a wink to be seeking the advice of "learned and unprejudiced" men who could help her "strain off what was personal and accidental . . . and so reach the pure fluid, the essential oil of truth" about women (25). What Woolf's "I" found were the writings of Professor von X in *The Mental, Moral, and Physical Inferiority of the Female Sex.*

The story Woolf's expert told about women is really a story of how experts become experts. The story is that women cannot discover or articulate the essential truth about what they are, because what they are is full of gaps created by the biases of personal consciousness. I said before that those gaps are sites of uncertainty and debate; it is there, at the gaps, that femaleness and femininity meet up with the other unreliable figures I have mentioned: the queer, the pervert, the insane, the feminist, those not authorized to tell their own story. Out of their lies, silence, or babble, the expert constructs the hopeful story of his own objective authority.

This hierarchical scenario is, however, oversimplified. LeVay is not only the scientist studying homosexuality, but as a gay man, a representative object of study. His statement about the ability of science to know everything about human sexuality is also a revelation of his potential to know himself. An acute observer like Woolf turns the arrangement to her own advantage, challenging Professor von X on his own ground, which is not the solid ground of objective science, but the shifting terrain occupied by those whose "I" has no real being. The expert and the object of study whose critique overturns him are both personas, but what "Woolf" has over the masculine expert is that hers is a conscious, purposeful production. Her persona is constructed out of the knowledge that "the essential oil of truth" about women is made of artificial ingredients.

Authenticity as Masquerade

Long before I took a B for my college literature paper, I had trouble with another assignment. A substitute teacher, the first male teacher I'd ever had, arrived in my fifth grade class on Valentine's Day and gave us the following assignment: the boys were to draw a picture of war and the girls were to draw a picture of love. The substitute wandered around the room, checking on the drawings. Although my head was full of images, they were all illicit. I could draw nothing. I began to panic.

I considered doing the boys' assignment instead, but I did not think he would let a girl get away with that. I was afraid of what he would do to me if I didn't come up with something that would look like love to him. The girl in front of me was drawing a bride and groom framed by a pink heart.

It would never have occurred to me that this was "love," but I dutifully copied it. What I drew was coarse and uncontrolled, the red method of war imposed on the pink ideal of heterosexual love. I was ashamed of the result. That is how the authorities caught up with me, in the form of a man vested with the power to demand an account of whom and how I loved.

It is easy to imagine what Morton Prince would say about this perverse story: there is nothing here worth knowing. And in fact, what I gave the substitute teacher was a child-sized version of what I would hope the adult pervert would proffer when forced to give an account of herself: a concealment, an image that might satisfy the interlocutor while giving away nothing real.

Something like that kind of concealment is what makes it possible for many unreliable narrators to get through their days. Joan Riviere's "Womanliness as a Masquerade" (1929) focused on the daily enactment of normative heterosexual femininity, but the predicament she describes is not limited to heterosexual women. "I shall attempt to show that women who wish for masculinity may put on a mask of womanliness to avert anxiety and the retribution feared from men." Except for the fact that masculinity was neither the object of my wishes nor a vehicle for satisfying my desires, Riviere might have been describing the situation of a queer ten-year-old girl. However, as Judith Butler (1993) remarked, homosexual desire has no place behind the mask Riviere dons. "Riviere would have us believe that this curious typological anomaly cannot be reduced to a repressed female homosexuality or heterosexuality. What is hidden is not sexuality, but rage" (52).

It makes sense that masquerading as "feminine" in order to avert retribution would make one angry, and anger would have been no more acceptable than ambition to the kind of heterosexual femininity Riviere spoke for. But what may have been concealed as well in Riviere's account was her own experience. An article exploring the confluence of personal and professional interests in Riviere's life found that her patient in "Womanliness as a Masquerade" resembled the psychoanalyst as she represented herself in private diaries (Hughes 1997). As I wrote this, I was looking for reasons to pretend that the incident with the substitute teacher happened to someone else. The risk in introducing autobiographical material is that it becomes more difficult to maintain the mask of authority, a mask already tricky for a woman to don because pretending to such authority testifies to a masculinity I (she) should not be able to have. Seeming to claim masculinity courts retribution from the experts, and even though the experts are just as inauthentic as those they judge, the consequences are quite real.

Given the risks, it makes sense that Riviere would pretend that her pretense of femininity was someone else's. The masquerade preserved her authoritative public persona, which she would have had to surrender had she identified herself with the object of her theorizing. That a mutually exclusive observer and object exist on opposite sides of a mediating lens is one of the common illusions that helps construct authority. Another illusion is to some extent perpetuated by both Riviere and Woolf: that the hierarchy of observer and object is reliably gendered such that one can depend upon the Professor von X's to be male, or if not male, at least masculine.

And so the authorities are quite a bit like the rest of us in having something to hide, but certain kinds of privilege make the cover-up more difficult to detect and the material consequences of detection less dreadful. Under such a regime, those who have been called to account for their queer sexuality before sexologists, judges, scientists, psychologists, teachers, neighbors, or parents would have few means of creating an authoritative account of their own lives. They could attempt to disappear, as I did in the fifth grade classroom, behind a mask of nothing-worthy-of-notice, or they could emerge, revealing their immodest selves to authoritative witnesses and taking the consequences.

One last proposition

Or there is another possibility, a way of navigating the gaps and shifting surfaces of sexuality without either disappearing entirely or presenting oneself for diagnosis. In *Shameless Propositions* I have followed this other way, using parody, subjective testimony, and a deconstructive strategy of following ostensibly reasonable arguments to their absurd ends. None of this competes for the kind of theoretical authority claimed by the multiple facsimiles of science I examine. There is plenty to be learned from tracking the experts as they look for ways to account for women's sexuality, but as far as I can tell, the real thing cannot be bottled. I am as glad of that as I was relieved to escape unnoticed on Valentine's Day.

In chapter 1, "Rats and Women," I begin with studies and experiments over the last forty years that try to identify material agents that might influence female sexual orientation and arousal. Scientists in endocrinology and genetics have proposed that females of various species will become "homosexual" if they are exposed to an excess of androgens during their development. The question of what such a transformation might really mean is interesting in itself, because what counts as real in the setting of sexual science is as unstable as one might expect given the already dizzying interrelationships among male, female, masculine, feminine, heterosexual, and homosexual. The proposition that females can be hormonally manipulated into behaving like males is enticing if it can be made to fit with the familiar story about how aggressive masculine agents, represented here in the male hormone and the scientist who delivers it, overwhelm the defenses of the vulnerable female. How well the scientific project fits with that narrative is more important than precision of terms (i.e., what exactly does it mean to be female, or to have a sexual orientation, when science shows how susceptible our anatomy and behavior are to the influence of hormones?) or whether the data generated support the original hypothesis. For those seeking to establish themselves as theoretical authorities, accuracy and results are in no way as important as cultural validity.

In the second chapter, "Being Perverse," I turn from endocrinology to psychoanalysis, and from homosexuality to its even more reprobate next of kin, perversion. Psychoanalysis has conventionally considered perversion a man's problem on the assumption that women lack the sexual agency, aggressive capacity, and genital anatomy necessary to execute a perversion. Authoritative accounts among psychologists, literary theorists, and historians often refer to the Marquis de Sade as the exemplary pervert, whose philosophy seeks to demolish civilization. Seduced by the vision of the pervert undermining social order, authoritative accounts of perversion gloss over evidence of extraordinary violence against women. The reason is simple: the social contract the pervert appears to violate does not prohibit such violence. To illuminate the social dynamics that continue to reproduce this apparently counterintuitive result, I turn to studies of authoritarian personality, which reveal why rape and other forms of violence against women continue to be tolerated despite decades of feminist activism.

Extending the discussion of perversion in chapter 3, "Sexually Offensive Women," I tackle the thinking of some dissenting psychoanalysts who have challenged the idea that perversion is a disorder of men. They find the idea of a sexually differentiated model more appealing. Included in the resulting laundry list of specifically female perversions are hostile maternal behaviors, eating disorders, and criminal behaviors including shoplifting and prostitution. These "female perversions" are of special concern because they are thought to perpetuate themselves in succeeding generations. A growing number of small criminological studies of female perpetrators refer to the new psychoanalytic models. Fueled in part by highly publicized anecdotal accounts of older women preying sexually on teenage boys, an idea is taking root: women are at once guilty of specific crimes and suffering from a generalized maternal pathology that can manifest in any unsettling behavior or disturbance of mind. Meanwhile, more conservative psychoanalysts engaged in the debate about the existence and nature of female perversion express fears about the negative effects of female homosexuality on species survival and produce a discourse of psychological eugenics replete with apocalyptic warnings about the barren world that will result if maternal perversions are allowed to reproduce themselves unchecked.

Insisting on a highly sexually differentiated model of perversion replicates the problems with the more traditional view that women are incapable of perversion. They share their worst features: the readiness to associate women's desire with social anarchy, the defensive denial of women's sexual agency, the eagerness to blame mothers for anything that goes wrong in the lives of their children, and the pernicious willingness to tolerate, refuse to see, or dismiss the effects of violence against women—which is, finally, part and parcel of the social contract that is supposed to prevent us from falling into chaos.

The disappointing outcome of inventing a whole world of perversions specific to women suggests one reason to support feminist and queer theorists' attempts to undermine binary structures of sexual difference. Despite their best efforts, however, anatomical and biological differences between male and female are still generally assumed to be the stable foundation of every sexual and familial relationship; further, they appear to engender the communities and larger scale political structures that perversion puts in peril. The idea that sexual difference is at its base heterosexual often goes unrecognized even in sophisticated discussions about the fluidity of gender and sexuality. In chapter 4, "Making Theoretical Space," I argue that it is possible to perceive the dominance of heterosexual forms without ascribing to them the power to determine the meaning of every meeting of lovers, family dynamic, or social relation. I introduce the polemical notion of "lesbian sexual difference" as a way to get at the root of the stubborn assumption that heterosexual pairings and their simulacra are the necessary foundation of social, sexual, and psychological order.

In the conclusion, the space I described in chapter 4 as opening up between women's status in the authoritative discourses on sexuality and their potential to perform as sexual agents becomes the space in which the most radical inventions of queer and feminist thinkers and activists can come to fruition. However, the passing fashion for considering queer and third wave feminism the postmodern and/or postfeminist solution to the failures of the second wave of feminism and "gay liberation" was brought about by means of the same authoritative gesturing that instated more conventional models of female sexuality. Postfeminist and post-LGBT narratives purport to reveal a projected or already accomplished end, describing the tribulations that necessitate that end and revealing the new beginning that follows it. The familiar rhetorical games queer and third-wave theorists play as they vie for authority against older models of feminist and LGBT liberation are dead ends. Only by questioning the meaning and behavior of theoretical authority can we open up new ground for constructing a more inclusive, less oppressive reality.

1
Rats and Women

Circulating testosterone values in [adult female] homosexual subjects averaged 38% higher than those in the heterosexual group.

—Nanette Gartrell

Interestingly, so far there has been more evidence that early androgens might play a role in homosexuality in women than in men.

—John Morris, Kyle Gobrogge, Cynthia Jordan, and S. Marc Breedlove

We cannot confidently say that hormones determine homosexual orientation.

—Karori Mbügua

Endocrine crimes

In 1952, British scientist Alan Turing was convicted on charges of gross indecency, or in other words, of having homosexual sex. He was ordered to receive injections of estrogen. His biographer Andrew Hodges remarked that Turing had attended a conference at which "P.B. Medawar had proposed a programme of experiments on male animals, injecting estrogen in order to reveal the neuro-physiological mechanism through the consequent alteration in behavior patterns. Rarely can a Fellow of the Royal Society [i.e., Turing] have had the honour of sitting at the wrong end of such an experiment" (474).

Turing's punishment reflects the most typical ways of conceiving the human/animal relation in studies like those Medawar proposed. The traditional vision of the scientist in his role as the brain and hands behind the experiment, taking as his object the homosexual condition represented in the body of the animal, folds under the ironic strain of a Fellow of the Royal Society taking the animal's place. Turing's punishment reveals that the proposition underlying studies like those Medawar planned has two parts. The first is openly acknowledged: animal studies can tell us something useful about how human beings respond to particular hormones. The second part, whether it is acknowledged or even consciously realized, is still with us over fifty years after Turing was penalized: what scientists learn from animal studies could be used to change the sexual responses, if not the sexual orientation, of human beings.

Turing's reversal of fortune opens other questions about the nature and distribution of authority, of who and what has the power to decide. Turing's only official punishment was hormonal, suggesting that estrogen was considered a singular or sovereign agent, sufficient to obliterate Turing's capacity for sexual expression and prevent further crimes. However, none of the changes in Turing's body and life could have occurred without the participation of the police and justice systems, the accumulating body of data on the action of hormones, the broader scientific community of which Turing was so prominent a member, and as Hodges's account makes apparent, the cooperation of Turing himself, his lover, and his family and friends.

In Turing's case, there were no functioning divisions between biological, scientific, and social forces; it took the authoritative weight of all the decision makers to bring about the strange apparition of a human being treated all too literally like a lab rat. Although the politics of sexuality has evolved, the nature of our institutions or of our selves have not changed since Turing's era.

Today it is far less acceptable to articulate the proposition that we might be able to change people's hormonal or even genetic status to produce a more uniformly sexed and gendered society. The proposition has not been lost, however. It is still apparent in current debates about what (if anything) should be done to direct the bodies and behavior of intersexed babies into categories of male and female, masculine and feminine. If it were similarly possible to identify babies who would grow up to be gay or lesbian, there would be a similarly impassioned debate about whether to "fix" them at once.

One of my students, formerly a counselor at a clinic that provided a full range of reproductive services, including abortion, occasionally fielded questions from newly pregnant women asking if the clinic could test for homosexuality. They wanted to schedule an abortion if the test was positive. Many who would, for whatever reason, abhor the idea of aborting a "gay baby" would nevertheless be glad to see genetic cures for homosexuality.

Biologist Ruth Doell, reviewing the evidence for biological explanations for sexual orientation, concluded that a "commitment to a belief in a biological mechanism . . . supports the hierarchy of power by those who benefit from that power" (27). Modern appeals for tolerance depend heavily on scientific authority, which these days tends to support two arguments: first, that homosexuality is inborn or determined very early in life, and second, that homosexuality is biologically too complex to be detected reliably by any method but self report or direct observation (and even then there is room for doubt).

The injections of estrogen Turing received could not cure homosexuality, but they could dull his ability to have sex and feminize his body. But what if the original hope had been fulfilled; what if injecting people with hormones made them heterosexual? And what if some modern alternative—gene "therapy," for instance, became available? At that point, scientific authority would evacuate arguments for tolerance.

The study at the heart of this chapter was conducted in the spirit of the experiment imposed on Turing, showing as well how hard it has been to let go of the hope that hormones could cure homosexuality. Günter Dörner's 1968 study "Hormonal Induction and Prevention of Female Homosexuality" divided female rats into several groups according to the number and timing of doses of hormones and the effects of those hormones on the organization and activation of the hypothalamus. The study posits a turnabout moment during fetal development when sexual orientation can be decisively changed.

The use of animals as models for women's sexuality helps to support that hierarchy of discursive and material authority that Doell referred to, but evidence of multiple forms of agency is woven throughout the evolving narratives of female sexuality in scientific discourse. In those narratives particular elements of the body and performance, including the clitoris, dominating behavior, and racial/species mixing, appear as contaminants of female heterosexuality.

Dörner likened the altered female rat's sexual behavior to the "distinctly male sexual behaviour" of women with untreated congenital adrenal cortical hyperplasia, suggesting thereby that the endocrine systems and sexual behavior of rats and humans are similar enough to make the rat a good analog for the human, and that human sexuality is polarized by masculine dominance and feminine submission (163).[1] Accepting that a close correspondence exists between rats and women, as Dörner's references to women invite one to do, means imagining women engaging not so much in masculine as unhuman-like patterns of sexual behavior. Similarly, John Money's reference to a "lesbian ewe," created by dosing the lamb fetus with androgens, suggests that the animal has violated behavioral expectations not only for her sex but also for her species (389). The "rat/woman" hybrid that emerges from animal models of women's sexuality is neither the triumphant successor to the scientific legacy nor its victim, but her body and her performances reveal much about the management of women's sexuality.

Many studies of female sexuality test the power of a sovereign agent that is genetic, psychological, or hormonal. In each of its various forms, the sovereign agent serves as the researcher's representative in the quest to manage sexual bodies and behaviors. The search for the sovereign agent shows that anxieties about women's sexuality continue to motivate research. At the end of the chapter, I come back to the question of who can serve as an authority and listen to one renegade voice speaking to the hybrid bodies and lives of sexual Others.

Managing rat sex

From the 1960s through the early 1990s, Dörner collaborated on numerous studies of homosexuality in rats, though only a few focus on female homosexuality.[2] In describing the impact of endocrinology on "queer science," Simon LeVay (1996) reported that Dörner considered homosexuality a "functional teratology" and "believed for many years that homosexuality was something to be cured or prevented" (118). The same belief made Alan Turing the unwilling successor to animal hormone research. Dörner himself went so far as to propose a program to measure hormone levels in women's amniotic fluid and make corrections if test results indicated her fetus might turn out to be homosexual. But by the early 1990s, Dörner's opinions had changed, and he asked the World Health Organization to declassify homosexuality as a mental disease (LeVay, 345, n. 8).

In the decades before Dörner's study was published, the possibility that homosexuality could be induced or prevented by the administration of hormones had been raised, debated, and at least occasionally rejected.[3] The debate continues, evolving (as Dörner's thinking did) in response to political and scientific shifts. One shift is that more attention is being given to the peripheral signs of androgen exposure; not only sexual or stereotypically gendered social behavior, but subtle physical differences, have been found to mark a lesbian difference. Two studies, one of finger length ratios (Breedlove et al. 1998) and one of click-evoked otoacoustic emissions in the cochlea (McFadden 2000), gained the attention of the popular media in the last few years; other studies followed, including one that found that mothers who smoked during pregnancy were more likely to have lesbian daughters, presumably by altering the fetuses' hormonal environment.[4]

The studies arrived at similar conclusions, finding that the cochleas, fingers, or prenatal histories of "homosexual women" were dissimilar to those of heterosexual women. The authors also hypothesized similar causes, positing that human female fetuses exposed to unusually high levels of androgens would tend to develop "masculinized" bodily features and behaviors. Using data gathered from self-identified lesbians, they correlated that hypothesized hormonal masculinization with homosexual desires.

There is no reason to think that McFadden and Breedlove (or any of the others) are interested in using their research to prevent homosexuality, and yet, I am concerned about the eugenic possibilities activated at the interface of sexuality with practical science, where normative heterosexual identities and behaviors can be encouraged to reproduce themselves and deviant identities and behaviors can be discouraged. If science advanced to the point where it was even marginally possible to identify subtly androgenized female fetuses who might grow up to have unfeminine fingers and queer desires, there are many who would be glad to prevent their births or give early treatment to try to prevent a lesbian outcome.

The animal studies advance us in that direction. Rats are only marginally comparable to women, but finding a credible likeness of bodies and behaviors isn't the point. Female rats in the laboratory are perfect analogs, not for women, but for the management of sexuality and gender. An effective study cooperates with the hope that it will be possible to manage sexual behavior through biological and technological means. The ongoing struggle to identify and modify particular sexual behaviors has profound consequences, especially for those who are most likely to be targeted for direct intervention.

Hybrids and other confusions

From a practical point of view, experimenting with animals and animal fetuses offers so many advantages over attempting to experiment directly on women and human fetuses that there is no question why Dörner and many others would have chosen the nonhuman alternative. One effect was to forge a kinship between the animal and the human, profitable for some humans but not for any animals, a relation in which the significant distinctions are those that determine which entities can be experimented on in particular ways, and which cannot. Donna Haraway claims a close relation to a mouse used for cancer research. "Oncomouse™ is my sibling, and more properly, male or female, s/he is my sister. Her essence is to be a mammal, a bearer by definition of mammary glands, and a site for the operation of a transplanted, human, tumor-causing gene—an oncogene—that reliably produces breast cancer." (1997, 79) The trademark symbol reminds the reader that Oncomouse was the first animal to be patented. The mouse is closely related to the human, not only because its body is engineered with a human gene to recreate a disease devastating to women, but because our medical, legal, and business institutions have called it into being.

Like breast cancer, homosexuality was "induced" in Dörner's rats so that it could be "prevented" in the human population. Neither I nor the rat benefit, but the connection can't be denied. Our sexualities are discursive and material productions, and our bodies have been called upon to account for our sexual behaviors. Given the histories of hormonal experimentation on queers of various kinds, I can perceive no clear distinction between rats and lesbians that would protect my kind from similar treatment. But there is one firm distinction: I will never be subjected to hormone experiments so that researchers can determine how to "prevent" homosexuality in rats. Another distinction is that the rat cannot participate discursively in the making of her sexuality any more than Oncomouse can speak to shape the meaning of her cancer. Their human analogues—women with breast cancer and lesbians—can do so.

The differences between the sexual behavior of rats and women drives another wedge into the cross-species sisterhood. Wendell Ricketts (1984) observes in a particularly astute critique that researchers' projects "have helped to make clear the absurdity of animal models of homosexuality," in part because they must account for sexual dimorphism in sexual behavior as well as the sex of the partner, a combination that does not translate well from animal to human models (85). Ricketts is correct that following animal/human analogies strictly to their conclusions produces an unworkable vision of both animal and human sex, but there are powerful reasons to ignore the problem.

Accounts of animal sexual behavior are impoverished precisely because they conform to unexamined fears and expectations about the human sexuality they are supposed to illuminate, and yet that impoverishment is highly effective in that it serves to maintain the order of things researchers share with the world beyond the lab. From the perspective of those who consider the prevention of homosexuality a worthy goal, the limits of Dörner's logic are not a measure of the success of the study. A better measure is the support it provides for heteronormative taxonomy of human sexuality, a hierarchy saturated with a Levitical suspicion of anything human that declines to be set apart according to a baffling but unrelenting division of matter and action into clean and unclean. This distinction becomes most apparent on the surface of the body, where various versions of the bad Other—unclean organic substances, unclean nonhuman species, unclean practices, and unclean human flesh—meet up with and may enter and become a part of a human body that can be purified by taking proper action. Proper action means following the law, resisting inducements to yield to the bad Other, admitting oneself for purification, and consenting to set oneself apart. Dörner' study is one small effort to maintain a screen between the category of unclean things into which rats fall (even heterosexual rats, but homosexual rats even more so) and the "female heterosexuality" that renders women fit for their proper reproductive role in the service of evolution.

Mary Douglas, in a study of abominations in Leviticus published at about the same time as Dörner's study of female homosexuality, identifies an order among the dietary laws that had eluded other interpreters: "In general the underlying principle of cleanness in animals is that they shall conform fully to their class. Those species are unclean which are imperfect members of their class, or whose class itself confounds the general scheme of the world" (1966, 55). Rats would be unclean because like mice they "perversely use their hands for walking," which engenders confusion in the proper order of locomotion (56).

Dörner's experiments engendered further confusion in an already unclean animal. Douglas implied that a rejection of hybridity and the equation of holiness with completeness motivated prohibitions on bestiality, incest, and adultery, but she did not analyze prohibitions on homosexuality.

However, female homosexuals would be unclean according to both the criteria she mentioned. It is at this point that the absurdity of the animal/human analogy evaporates. The analogy of female homosexuals to fetally androgenized rats—a relation that I will consider a conceptual hybridity with material consequences—has its roots in a religious sense of order set forth millennia before Dörner's experiments. Lesbians appear to be imperfect members of their class because they do not "complete" themselves by having reproductive sex with men. If participation in sanctioned heterosexual reproduction defines women as a class, lesbians are not fully women. Furthermore, lesbians perversely use their hands, tongues, and devices rather than penises. From the Levitical point of view, and from Dörner's as well, they are using the wrong equipment with the wrong sexual partners to no good purpose. Such behavioral abominations could only be compounded by abominations of reproduction and embodiment. "Hybrids and other confusions are abominated," Douglas wrote; therefore, "You shall not let your cattle breed with a different kind; you shall not sow your field with two kinds of seed" (Leviticus 19:19, quoted in Douglas, 53.) Borderline cases are not clean, in part because their relationship is too partial and too complex to be easily understood, and the rat/woman hybrid that begins to emerge from Dörner's study is such a case.

The "nature/nurture" debate that continues to dominate our sexual politics is a competition between "hard" biological science and "soft" social science. The terms are classically gendered: men conquer nature, which is feminine, while women provide nurture. The division seeks to avoid the awful fusion of unlike things (hard and soft sciences, masculinity and femininity) in favor of a clean separation and hierarchy of influences. Observations regarding the "plasticity" of women's sexuality suggest that it doesn't occupy any cleanly defined category, and that might be cause for concern. Women's flexibility could make them seem more dangerous (because less predictable), more exciting (because more open to possibility), or more vulnerable to cultural influences and more amenable to meeting others' sexual needs than men are. The last interpretation of women's sexual plasticity is the one that rises to the top.[5] The ability to change means something different when it is found in a woman than it would in a man; in her, it is a sign of feminine submission, and that is what makes it tolerable in the Levitical sense, in a man, it would be a sign of masculine agency. Thinking of women's sexual behavior as self-directed and coming from within rather than as a response to an external demand would disrupt the categories to a distressing extent, so much so that a woman with a strong, narrowly directed, and unchanging sexual drive would have to be considered masculine. If she could be found to be under the influence of androgens, however, the potential threat is averted, and the qualities of feminine submission and masculine assertion go back to their respective corners.

Almost three decades after Dörner, neuroanatomist Simon LeVay (1993), whose study of the hypothalamus is among the most cited and controversial attempts to locate and measure homosexual difference, reaffirmed with jaunty confidence the sovereign explanatory power of biology, predicting that the answer "will be figured out by biologists, and it will be figured out a lot sooner than most people imagine" (29). Biologists, LeVay contended, will provide not only explanations, but the means to either eradicate or "conserve" homosexuality: "Once we have the human species in a bottle, dissected, labeled, catalogued and explained in all its delightful and repellent diversity, we will need to decide: What do we want from this particular animal? What shall we conserve, and what shall we discard? I think it would be nice to keep gays and lesbians, but why should I expect people to agree with me? I shouldn't, unless I can persuade them that we're worth keeping" (29).

Some of those on the "soft" side of the sciences, by contrast, have insisted on the nonhierarchical interdependence and inseparability of biological and psychological influences on gender, including characteristics of masculinity and femininity that have been used to differentiate sexual orientations. For instance, Breedlove (1994), a psychologist in the Neuroscience Program at Michigan State University who participated prominently in the finger length studies, began a discussion of sex differentiation by emphasizing that we should not treat biological and social influences "as if these were separable forces" (309) and emphasizes that existing genetic studies deal in statistical probabilities.

Expressing a similar idea in a book about cognitive differences between the sexes, Diane Halpern, former president of the American Psychological Association, wrote, "Nature and nurture are like conjoined (Siamese) twins who share a common heart and nervous system. How could we ever decide where one twin ends and the other begins?" (2000, 10). No matter her intentions, Halpern's choice of metaphor undermined her argument that nature and nurture only make sense if considered as one organism: historically, conjoined twins were classed as "monsters," unholy mixtures of bodies that should never have become one. Even now, few would disagree that twins are vastly better off born separately than conjoined. The implication is that until we can disentangle our pure nature from its messy social and psychological effects we will not be in control of our human destiny.

For most, that destiny (which is synonymous with our survival) is imperiled by any data that undermine the mutually reinforcing distinctions between masculine and feminine, heterosexual and homosexual, and dominant and submissive. From a heteronormative perspective, the female homosexual is a profound threat unless she can be accounted for within existing distinctions, and that is why she must appear to be a usurper or imitator of masculinity, at least when she has sex.

Rat agency

Generalizing from rats to mammals, Dörner stated, "the direction of the sex instinct is completely determined—independently of the genetic sex—by the androgen level during the critical hypothalamic differentiation phase" (164). The sex of the partner and the preference for dominant or submissive sexual behavior together compose the mammalian "sex instinct." Genes do not participate in inducing and preventing female homosexuality. For the sake of Dörner's goal, this is probably just as well, as genetic engineering to induce or prevent homosexuality would present technical difficulties that have yet to be surmounted.

The alternative Dörner offers is a female sexuality determined entirely by the sovereign action of androgens. In practice, however, the sexualities in Dörner's taxonomy are not produced by androgens acting of their own accord; in fact, what makes androgens useful is that they do not take independent action, but work in partnership, as one crucial member of a complex apparatus that produces the sex instinct in all its permutations and, ultimately, makes the female a docile participant in the evolutionary narrative.

This apparatus includes not just the injected hormone, but the network of researcher, protocol, lab, and research institution, all acting on female rat fetuses to direct their development. It also includes things less concrete: a technologically assisted homosexuality (i.e., bad desire) and inappropriate gender role (i.e., female masculinity) taking over the heterosexual female body. Thus the apparatus is a composite of material and theoretical entities and nonhuman/human agents, and the scope of its agency is determined by (a) the extent to which a rat's anatomy and behaviors can respond to androgens, and (b) the concepts of sexual and reproductive order that guide the research program.

It is difficult to recognize the efficacy of the rat in this apparatus, in part because Dörner's rhetoric gives all power to androgens, and in part because Dörner fails to take account of the limits rat anatomy and physiology place on what data can be produced. I would say that it makes sense to consider those constraints as a form of agency.

I have already associated hybridity with uncleanness, so describing rats as part of the sex study apparatus implicates Dörner in the perversion of the rat/human mix. He resists—remaining properly "set apart" according to both Levitical and scientific standards—by means of rhetorical strategies that make androgens sovereign agents and discourage the question of rat agency.

The often bitter politics the rat sex study engages with make responsibility or even blame the most salient aspects of sexual agency; scientists who pretend they are standing apart from all that, no matter whether they interpret their data to support "pro" or "anti" homosexual arguments, are attempting to do the impossible: absolve themselves of political agency.

According to a rudimentary definition, an agent can act or exercise power in various ways. Dörner explicitly assigned agency to androgens, but in making that assignment and calling the behaviors he observed "homosexual," he was himself exercising political as well as intellectual agency.[6] Hormones influence anatomy and behavior in ways that can be measured and expressed as probabilities, but they do not produce states of being like homosexuality.

The scientist who interpreted the data and announced conclusions seems to be the *only* agent in the rat sex study that could induce or prevent homosexuality. Certainly the rat/woman hybrid, who is represented as robotically controlled by hormones, does not figure even as a potential agent. She is hardly even a material entity. In her place, we are offered "female homosexuality," a state, an orientation, a set of behaviors, not a thing at all, and still less a subject. And yet, the humans and rodents in question do take action, making behavioral choices just like scientists do, within the constraints imposed by their environments and the biological limits of their brains and bodies.

The title "Induction and Prevention of Female Homosexuality" promises a decisive and sustainable division between homosexuality and heterosexuality, as well as a formula for removing females from the deviant category and replacing them squarely within the normal category. If no recognizable aspect of female sexuality escapes the determining influence of hormones, females lack sexual volition. There is every reason to believe that if this is true for females, it must be true for males, but similar phenomena mean different things depending on genetic sex—even though, according to the narrative Dörner follows, genes do not participate in the production of sexuality. Working in conjunction with femininity, complete subjection to hormones is evidence of a deep passivity that underlies the appearance of self-directed action. Males' relation to androgens is different; if under the influence they are more aggressive and sexually powerful, it is not because they are passively in the hormone's power. They are doing what comes naturally to them as men.

The story for the genetic female is quite different. As long as a female exhibits qualities associated with femininity and maternity, the question of volition need not arise. However, when her behavior appears to bring her into conflict with femininity, the possibility arises of a female directing her own action. The exercise of will on the part of the female upsets the order of things. Dörner's conclusion—that the rat's dominating behavior is really the result of the masculinizing action of androgens over which she can exert no control—restores a sense of order. Nothing a female can do—including such clear transgressions as the performance of acts of sexual dominance and the achievement of physical sexual pleasure with other females—finally exceeds or violates what can come about within the conjoined system of mammalian endocrinology and laboratory experiment.

A female might appear to be choosing sex objects and acting to satisfy a sexual urge, but the system is really running her. When the experimental apparatus intercedes to prevent her homosexuality, she will be heterosexual. When she is heterosexual, nothing in her behavior will seem to be out of order, and there will no longer be anything to gain in observing her; her internal hormonal balance will be observant. It is not heterosexuality per se, but the docility of her body under the determining influence of androgens that the experimental apparatus makes evident.

Dörner's data, however, indicate that it is not reasonable to leave so little room to consider the female—at this point, either rat or woman—as an agent. Dörner's experimental design and the data he ends up with provide evidence that the rats violated the order of sexualities Dörner used to evaluate his data. Dörner divided his female rats into several groups according to the number and timing of doses of hormones and the effects of those hormones on the organization and activation of the hypothalamus. He achieved results that ranged from predominately homosexual behavior, in which female rats treated just after birth and as adults mounted other rats twenty-one times for every nine times they allowed themselves to be mounted, to complete homosexual behavior, in which females treated with androgens prenatally and postnatally mounted other rats and "showed ejaculatory-like behavioural patterns" during every sexual encounter (164).

Another experimental group of rats represented the possibility of "preventing" homosexuality. In these rats, Dörner "induced" homosexuality with androgens but "prevented" it by giving anti-androgens concurrently. The "prevention of homosexuality" group only mounted other rats twelve times for every twenty-five times they allowed themselves to be mounted, a pattern similar to that of untreated female rats assumed to represent heterosexuality. The rats' lack of concern about the sex of the rats they engage with sexually means that rats cannot be made to fit the common sexual categories Dörner employs; the behaviors of androgenized females fail to support his contention that androgens are completely responsible for determining the direction of the mammalian sex instinct.

The research proceeds from the assumption that mutually exclusive categories of female heterosexuality and homosexuality exist and can be mapped onto a framework for evaluating which bodies should exhibit sexual submissiveness and which should assume dominance. That assumption breaks down in part because there is no effective correspondence between the sexual identity categories and the framework, but it also fails because rat sex deals in ratios rather than absolute categories into which entire, identifiable groups could fall. Endowed with different assumptions and a different interpretive emphasis, Dörner's data could be used to deconstruct common assumptions about sexuality.

The definition of homosexuality as a phenomenon completely antithetical to heterosexuality; its depiction as something that can be induced and prevented; the insistence on the all-powerful action of androgens in producing sexuality—these all-or-nothing rhetorical productions are tightly interdependent. If any one of them can be challenged successfully, the rhetorical apparatus fails. If heterosexuality and homosexuality are not mutually exclusive, then homosexuality is not a discrete state of being or set of behaviors that can be induced and prevented; if androgens (or some other sovereign agent) do not function to determine the object of sexual desire and a clean division of dominance and subordination, then homosexuality and heterosexuality cannot be thought of as mutually exclusive, and homosexuality can neither be induced nor prevented by the action of a sovereign agent.

What affects Dörner's thinking about sexuality is an inability to think of the rat as an agent in relation to her sexual behaviors. It's not that he is unable to attribute agency to something nonhuman; androgens are granted a highly powerful agency. It is rats that despite their complex organization have the status of passive objects. To use Bruno Latour's phrasing, objective material entities "just stand there, unproblematically composed of forces, of atoms, of elements" (1994, 8). This is the rat. Androgens move through the rat, taking action, directing the sexual instinct, making behavior; without androgens, the rat would just stand there, sexually speaking. The rat is neither a subject with free will nor a sovereign nonhuman agent, so it is difficult to perceive her acting at all.

Karen Barad's discussion of nonhuman agency suggests a foundation for defining a kind of "ratly agency." "From a humanist perspective," she wrote, "the question of nonhuman agency may seem a bit queer, since agency is generally associated with issues of subjectivity and intentionality. However, if agency is understood as an enactment and not something someone has, then it seems not only appropriate but important to consider nonhuman and cyborgian forms of agency as well as human ones" (1998, 112). The association of human and nonhuman agency is closer yet because the rats' enactments—their performances of "dominant" and "submissive" sex—cannot be extricated from the intentions and interpretations of the human subjects who undertake and fund this kind of research, along with those who come along and critique it. Although Barad included in her elaboration of agential realism the crucial recognition that agency is as much at work when "apparatuses are primarily reinforcing" as it is amid "a 'clash' of apparatuses," ratly agency is more easily detected when the rat takes some action not already accounted for by the researcher.

For instance, a rat can learn and bring what it learns to bear on the apparatus that affects her sexuality. Dörner noted that his extremely homosexual female rats lack vaginas; he also observed that they show "ejaculatory-like behavioural patterns," but he did not comment further on the structure of their genitalia (164). The rats may also have had enlarged clitorises.[7] Anne Fausto-Sterling suggested that anatomy influences rats' learning about mounting behavior and sexual pleasure (224). Mothers lick the genitals of male pups, but not those of females. This maternal behavior affects the male's sexual development. If Dörner's newborn female rats had enlarged clitorises, did their mothers lick them and so encourage a more male-typical sexual development?

The point is not to favor nurture over nature. Social and biological phenomena interact so closely that it makes little sense to distinguish them.

What is significant—and too often downplayed in discussions of sexuality—is that if a rat can learn things that have a direct impact on her sexual behavior, then she is an actor in the system. It would be as inaccurate to say she is a manipulable object at the mercy of hormones as it would be to say that she has free will and acts only by choice.

She is not purely one thing or the other, but a hybrid integrated in a larger system that does not function unless she takes action. The actions she takes can be predicted statistically, and she can only act within certain parameters, but even a rat cannot be depended on to do the same thing every time she is presented with, for instance, another rat willing to be mounted. The uncertainties about what she will do are minor, however, compared with the uncertainties about what it means when an androgenized female rat mounts or declines to mount, or offers herself for mounting to, another female or male rat.

Dörner's references to women and mammals as a class suggest that when it comes to sex rats and women occupy nearby positions in a sexual taxonomy. Because researchers experiment on rats to find out things about women (and not the reverse), we are meant to read from rats to women: if rats are merely passive recipients of all-powerful hormonal regulation that induces and prevents female homosexuality, then to some very significant degree women must be as well.

Right now, forty years after Dörner's experiments, hormonal explanations for human behavior are more popular than ever, at least among my students, most of whom are in their early twenties. In my classes, I have heard women make all of the following interrelated claims:

1) When women behave erratically or cruelly to their friends, they have premenstrual syndrome. PMS makes women undependable, which explains why men occupy most positions of responsibility.
2) Men are hormonally driven to compete. Some women like to compete too, but not as much as men because most women opt for motherhood.
3) Women become mothers because they have a hormonally powered "maternal instinct" that makes them want to have babies. The same hormones that make women want to have babies gives them the ability to provide good child care.
4) Men, however, lack the right hormones for maternal behavior, so they are likely to forget to feed their children or put diapers on backward.
5) In place of maternal hormones, men have hormones that make them need a lot of sex and give them the muscles to overpower a woman, so rape will always be with us.

Perhaps the only claim missing is that sexual orientation is determined by hormones. Students usually believe that lesbians and gay men have normal hormones, just like heterosexual people. For them it is genes, not hormones, that determine sexual orientation. Students are not usually prepared to say anything about how genes act to influence sexual orientation (for instance, by influencing the timing and balance of hormones the body produces), any more than they can say how genes give a person blue or brown eyes.

One of the conclusions to be drawn from listening to students talk about how human biology influences our aptitudes and social/sexual behavior is that science education in the United States leaves a great deal to be desired, but of even greater concern is their willingness to abdicate agency, to accept that we are helpless in the face of our hormones or our genes. Recently some students told me about a study they heard about in another class that proved femininity and masculinity are natural, not learned. In this experiment, they said, a researcher found that young male monkeys preferred boy toys, and young female monkeys preferred girl toys. The list of questions they could not answer about the experiment is long. They did not know, for a start, who had performed the experiment, where the results were published, what kind of monkeys were used, what toys they had been given to play with, how the researcher measured a monkey's preference for one toy over another, or whether preferences were radically or mildly differentiated by sex. What mattered was that boys were boys and girls were girls, even if the boys and girls were monkeys.

It would be tempting to conclude that my students, handicapped by naïveté and youth, are more willing than most people to accept partial and distorted knowledge as long as it affirms what they have heard before and accepted as true. However, their ideas reflect quite faithfully the kinds of questions that science has been interested in asking about gender. Lawrence Summers, whose comments about the limits of women's ability to do math and science kicked up a highly public fuss in 2005, told a brief story about his daughters, one of whom, when given trucks to play with, referred to the smaller truck as the baby and the bigger truck as the daddy truck, which Summers seems to have taken as proof that nothing can stop a little girl from being feminine; given trucks to play with, a little girl will fail to use them as a boy would.

The truck anecdote was picked up by the *New York Times*, the *Washington Post*, the *Boston Globe*, *Slate*, the *Eagle Forum*, and Weblogs too numerous to mention, but like my students' monkey story, it was strangely irrelevant to the issues at hand. It would appear that his bright toddler was able to use herself, her father, and small and large trucks to draw analogies of size, surely a hopeful sign for any parent who would like his child to do well at math. However, the story reveals nothing as remarkable as an inborn sense of gender.

Gender in these stories is an abstraction so dissociated from the material scene that it achieves a mystical status. The emergent rat-woman hybrid inhabits that reality as well. She has the general form of the human and female, but the sexuality is more rodentlike. How would she behave, if she were real? If left untreated or put through the complete induction-and-prevention process, she would usually have sex with heterosexual men who like to dominate. But she would also have occasional sex with lesbians (hybrids who, like the rats in Dörner's experiment, have been exposed to abnormally high concentrations of androgens prenatally or postnatally), other heterosexual women, or homosexual men. What would make these women heterosexual is not only their (admittedly nonexclusive) preference for sex with men, but their typically submissive sexual behaviors, which tend to facilitate conception and pregnancy. They fail to comply fully with Levitical sanctions against hybridity and homosexuality, but to a lesser degree than exclusive lesbians. In practical terms these heterosexual women still count as normal enough to be placed in the control group, but their behaviors don't support a fastidious division of heterosexuality from homosexuality.

Dörner's extremely androgenized rats—I've just been calling them "lesbians" in their hybrid form—are analogs for what right-wing psychoanalysts call "compulsory female homosexuals," meaning that they do not submit sexually to males (nor, indeed, to anyone). Following the analogy to its conclusion, compulsory female homosexuals, helpless to resist the determining influence of the extra androgens that have reshaped their hypothalamuses, genitals, and sexual desires, would not be able to have satisfactory sex with others like themselves; instead, they would be driven to mount any sexually compliant object, including bisexual and heterosexual women and what Dörner refers to as "homosexual males," a label earned because of their abnormal willingness to take up a submissive position during sex with either male or female rats. The categories of sexual orientation Dörner has been using are not powerful enough to sort out this heady admixture of deviant bodies and promiscuous behavior. For the rat/woman hybrid, nothing seems to be compulsory except the division of entities into categories of dominance or submission.

A DOMINATING CLITORIS

The categories Dörner is using cannot ultimately support his findings, but the fault for that does not rest wholly with him. His use of "heterosexuality" and "homosexuality" in relation to the rat/woman hybrid recapitulates a long tradition of efforts to describe and manage female sexuality—a tradition that continues today in forms only superficially different from those that came before, as the finger length and cochlea studies indicate. I can't attempt a full account of that history, but will establish a few links.

It is possible to see, in the classical Greek system of sexual relations David Halperin (1993) described, traces of a similar reluctance to confront the prospect of women abandoning a submissive, heterosexual position in order to gratify themselves directly. In that ancient system, what mattered most was how participants related to one another on a hierarchy of social and sexual dominance and submission. Halperin recommended against considering this a "sexuality," and instead described it as "a sociosexual discourse structured by the presence or absence of its central term: the phallus" (421). Only adult male citizens were always expected to assume sexual dominance over others. Women, boys, slaves, and foreigners could only take up submissive positions relative to this superior class. Although Halperin addressed male perspectives, it appears that of those contained in the category of partners to be penetrated, only women were always positioned for social and sexual compliance. Boys could grow up, either to be adult male citizens, or at least—as male slaves and foreigners—to have some submissive bodies, positioned even lower on the hierarchy, available to them. In such a system, female sexual aggression would have been perceived—assuming it could be perceived at all—as a gross contradiction. In a footnote, Halperin reported that the aggressive "tribad" with an "overdeveloped clitoris" already exists in the classical context, but he believed she was "a long-lived fictional type," not a real sexual agent (429).

The sexual ordering system of the ancient Greeks speaks to the situation of the extremely androgenized female rat/woman, a fictional type come to life at last. For her, as for the Greek citizen, the sex of the object is merely a matter of taste or availability; what is compulsory is her positioning as the dominant—penetrating—partner. However, the notion of female sexual dominance is as troublesome to the schema of binary sex difference that underlies the rat sex study as it would have been to the ancient system. In particular, Dörner's use of concepts of sexual dominance and submission to formulate female sexual categories hints at a perception of the lesbian as an omnivorous sexual predator, fearsome because she could victimize hormonally weakened or metaphorically castrated men, either indirectly by commandeering their women, or directly by forcing them into sexual submission.

Certain features of the rat sex study accorded with the nineteenth-century concept of inversion, for which a contrary sex instinct—evident in assertive desires and behaviors that seemed to the scientific observer appropriate to the opposite sex—proved a more riveting transgression than the choice of a same-sex partner.[8] A female invert was another hybrid type who preferred relatively "normal," conventionally feminine women who, like heterosexual rats, are willing to submit. Julian Carter (1997) quoted one of Ellis's correspondents who asserted a shared understanding of the meaning of sexual difference: "the difference in gender, and the very definite contrast between the *normal* male and the *normal* female merely results from the orderly process of evolution" (161). The order of distinctions that divides the unclean from the clean in Leviticus was here reworked in the joining of scientific and moral concerns about *normal* and *abnormal*. The bad Other, *abnormal*, was intermixed with those who failed to maintain "a very definite contrast" between male and female. The invert would fail to display what Havelock Ellis described as "that sexual shyness and engaging air of weakness and dependence which are an invitation to men," the human response corresponding to the rat's lordosis (Ellis, 98). Like the androgenized female rat, the female invert attracted weak and effeminate males because of her masculine tendency to dominate. Carter demonstrated brilliantly the linkage of abnormal sexual expression with the primitive and nonwhite. "The sexology of the normal, the achievements of civilization beyond the prehistorical stages, and the ability to make distinctions are here linked in ways that help to entangle savagery and perversion with the tendency to confuse separate entities" (Carter, 163). The invert and other sex/gender deviants were significant not in themselves but because of what they demonstrated about the success of evolution in producing an ever more stable taxonomy of race and sex, a taxonomy necessary to the production of civilization. The white invert's inability to distinguish male from female generalized to racial distinctions. No longer set apart by her whiteness, she fell back down the evolutionary line toward a primitivism represented in people of color—who, especially if inverted, signified more acutely the enfolding of racial and sexual disorder with nonwhiteness.

Though the invert eventually lost currency, giving way to a lesbian figure defined less by transgressive gender performance and deviant body shape and more by same-sex object choice, we continue to live with the legacy of those diligent efforts to discover the physical mark that would allow interested parties to identify the homosexual. Studies through the 1990s continued to differentiate lesbians from heterosexual women according to body build, choice of masculine or feminine clothing, and hormonally influenced phenomena such as menarche and premenstrual syndrome.[9]

The persistence of concerns about the shape and functioning of the lesbian body leads me to consider another component of the rat/woman hybrid: How do the potential effects of "extra" androgens on the genitals of genetically female rats (and by analogy, the bodies of lesbians) enter into definitions of sexual orientation? Concerns about the size and agency of the clitoris have a long history, as suggested by Valerie Traub's fine analysis of seventeenth-century representations of women's genital anatomy in which "the clitoris and the 'tribade' are positioned paratactically as mutually constitutive forms of female matter" (1995, 314). Tribadism was defined primarily by behavior in which women locked their thighs together in order to rub their clitorises. The tribade represented an unholy mixture of feminine and masculine body and behavior. During the "clitoral 'age of discovery,'" a discourse evolved "that increasingly fixated on the clitoris as the disturbing bodily emblem of female erotic power" (309). Amputation of the clitoris—if it was large enough to make the male physician uncomfortable—was suggested as a cure.

The experts confidently associated deviant anatomy and transgressive sexual behavior with racial "others"; if a white woman were to possess a large clitoris or use it for her own or another woman's pleasure, the association would work very much like the rat/woman hybrid, to drag the white woman down to a more primitive level.

Margaret Gibson (1997) picked up the threads of the discourse on clitoral hypertrophy, focusing on the end of the nineteenth century, when doctors associated "nymphomania," masturbation, and sexual inversion in women with enlarged clitorises and an excess of sexual energy. This was especially true for the female invert, whose sexuality was characterized by violent "attacks of sexual furor" and attempts to physically overpower other women or get them drunk enough to submit to "orgies of tribadism" (123).

According to Gibson, fewer doctors in the late nineteenth century recommended clitoridectomy for homosexuality. The milder treatments they favored, such as douches or baths, seem to have been designed to reduce sexual aggression rather than to obliterate desire. Race continued to form an essential part of the network of forces producing deviance, as Siobhan Somerville (1994) confirmed by citing nineteenth- and early twentieth-century commentary on the genital anatomy of African, African American, and inverted women. Observers discovered once more abnormally large clitorises, enlarged inner labia, or scrotumlike outer labia (26–29).

In her comprehensive examination of modern scientific readings of the homosexual body in the United States, Jennifer Terry (1999) demonstrated that concerns about the bodies of lesbians persisted and continued to be associated with race as a determinant of sexual deviance. The most compelling passages Terry cited are quotes from women who consented to participate in a study by the Committee for the Study of Sex Variants in the 1930s. For instance, Myrtle, a black performer in vaudeville, whetted the researchers' interest by pointing out that with her enlarged clitoris, she could give women so much pleasure they would leave their husbands. Susan, an African American woman who also delighted her lovers with her large clitoris, felt that her endowment meant she "should take the active part" with her female lovers (Terry, 242–43). Terry concluded that the interviews and gynecological examinations heightened the anxieties of male researchers involved in the study, one of whom tried to prove by means of a diagram that a clitoris, even a large one, could not satisfy a partner (Henry, 1128).

The rat sex study emerged into a history of scientific investigation of women's sexuality marked, from first to last, by anxiety about the power of women's sexual capacities and the fear that heterosexual intercourse might not satisfy women's desires. Mary Jane Sherfey's treatise on female sexuality (1966), drawing on the work of Masters and Johnson, was published two years before Dörner's study. Sherfey, a psychiatrist who had studied with Alfred Kinsey, intended to do research on the sexual responses of women and other primates. One of her missions was to put to rest the shopworn Freudian notion that a woman must give up active, masculine, clitoral pleasure and locate her orgasms in her vagina.

In her "Primer on Sexual Anatomy," Sherfey included a drawing of female sexual anatomy superimposed on the analogous area in the male, remarking that "the penile and clitoral systems are exact homologues of each other" (155). Thomas Laquer quoted Galen (ca. 130–200) saying much the same thing: "You could not find a single male part left over that had not simply changed its position" in the design of the female anatomy (5).

When considering the meaning of female sexual pleasure, both Sherfey and Laquer cited the myth in which Hera blinded Tiresias when s/he agreed with Zeus that women experience more sexual pleasure than men (Laquer, 4; Sherfey, 165). In his concluding paragraph, Laquer noted that the evolution of scientific knowledge eventually produced "new discursive wars" in which "feminists as well as antifeminists sacrificed the idea of women as inherently passionate" in order to place women where they thought they belonged in social and familial hierarchies (35). Sherfey entered those interminable wars to fight for her conviction that women are indeed sexually passionate, but she remained firmly in the antifeminist camp, abandoning logic to argue that while Zeus possessed "a wisdom far beyond that bourne of time and place," Hera is "the original militant women's libber," willing to do violence to anyone who opposes her conviction that women are sexually *inferior* to men (165).

The impact of Sherfey's political positioning was most evident, however, when she speculated on the consequences of female sexual potency. She made an argument similar to that of nineteenth-century sexologists for considering women's desire a potentially dangerous artifact left over from our prehistory, contending that "it is conceivable that the *forceful* suppression of women's inordinate sexual demands was a prerequisite to the dawn of every modern civilization and almost every living culture. Primitive women's sexual drive was too strong, too susceptible to the fluctuating extremes of an impelling, aggressive erotism to withstand the disciplined requirements of a settled family life . . . Constant infant care would be out of the question" (138). Modern woman, on the other hand, eschews her own immoderate sexual desire, and with it the intense orgasms she could have through "masturbation," in order to enjoy "the warmth of sexual relations, however mild the orgasms, with a loved one" during heterosexual intercourse in a monogamous relationship (162).

Sherfey's vision of sexual pandemonium and the feminine compromises that saved us from it took account only of women's heterosexual desire. The (averted) threat that women might refuse to give up their own passions in the service of evolutionary progress reproduced the old narrative in which an excessive sexuality unites with a racially determined female primitivism. That marriage produced as its hybrid progeny the sexually aggressive female homosexual in her rodent and human forms.

According to the conventional narrative of species progress, evolution acts upon the body to make it serviceable in heterosexual intercourse. Geoffrey Miller (1998) asserted that only evolutionary theory could provide a satisfactory answer to the question "Why have males always dominated political, economic, and cultural life in every known society?" (118). His answer contained some significant "ifs": "if most economic behavior is mating effort by males to acquire material resources for attracting and provisioning females, and if most cultural behavior is male mating effort to broadcast courtship displays to multiple female recipients, then cultural dimorphism [i.e., male dominance] is easily explained by sexual selection" (118) According to this kind of theory, every aspect of being human—everything from art (in Miller's view, only men produce significant art) to the ability of women to have orgasms—is driven by the exigencies of heterosexual mate choice. It is not just that we have to have sufficient heterosexual intercourse to reproduce ourselves. Human beings, according to this view, are only reproductively successful because men dominate women. If male-dominated heterosexuality failed, what could follow but the end of civilization as we know it?

Female aggression is the force that would topple it all. Sherfey spoke directly to the fear that there could be something animal-like and primitive in women, something beyond the reach of civilized control, something that—most monstrously—might make a male's mate choice irrelevant. Sherfey assured her readers that modern woman was committed to supporting civilization from beneath, but Dörner offered stronger reassurances. His study responded to the fear of female aggression by subsuming it under the name of an abnormal, but preventable, female sexuality. The essential argument was that biology itself—the laws of evolution and the sovereign power of androgens—could be relied on to prevent the ultimate disaster from materializing.

I don't share those fears; instead, I worry about the negative effects of giving them free reign. The woman's body that could produce anatomical and behavioral deviances powerful enough to undo the civilizing effects of socialization and hormone regulation would be far more mixed (up) than the body of the androgenized rat. As the findings of sexologists fueled anxieties about oversexed and deviantly gendered females, the "sexual revolution" was underway and feminism was again on the rise. John D'Emilio and Estelle Freedman cite Anne Koedt's 1969 essay "The Myth of the Vaginal Orgasm," which used data from Kinsey and Masters and Johnson to reason that "the recognition of the clitoral orgasm would threaten the heterosexual *institution.*" Its demolition is precisely what Sherfey feared would happen if women were not prevented from indulging their endless capacity for orgasm (313).

The "Induction and Prevention of Female Homosexuality" speaks to this trouble: the most compelling reason for a researcher to learn how to induce female sexual dominance (i.e., a masculinized form of sexual expression, or homosexuality) is to learn how to prevent it. What the rat sex researchers induced and prevented was the "liberation" of female sexuality from male dominance.

On whose authority?

> I would like to enter a woman the way any man can, and to be entered —to leave and to be left—to be hot and hard and soft all at the same time in the cause of our loving. I would like to drive forward and at other times to rest or be driven.
>
> —Audre Lorde, *Zami: A New Spelling of My Name*

Researchers at the turn of the twenty-first century make fewer direct references to the prevention or control of female homosexuality, but studies of hormones and sexual orientation continue, usually updated with reference to genetic influences and brain structure. Few conclude that hormones are sovereign agents influencing sexual orientation, but those who critique hormone studies don't receive much attention.[10] Late twentieth-century lesbian and gay activism helped to change the discourse and brought harassment and discrimination of lesbians, gay men, bisexuals, and transgendered people into the open, but there is no way to know if these hard-won changes have taken root deeply. A study of psychologists' methods found that approximately 11 percent still favor using psychotherapy to change sexual orientation, and almost 6 percent favor using aversion "therapy," a practice promoted especially for gay men during the 1960s, involving emetic solutions and electric shock (Jordan 1995). Though the methods differ depending on the discipline, the expectation is the same: to "prevent" or cure deviant behaviors and identities.

This helps to explain why the measure of Dörner's success cannot be taken with reference to his study's coherence. What matters is that the questions Dörner wanted to answer find much direct support from other studies about sexuality. The study recycles elements of that history without attempting to create an internally consistent account. Such an account would have undermined the rat/woman analogy and made critiques like those of Ricketts and Fausto-Sterling unnecessary. Thus the absurd turns in the account of rat/woman sex are grounded in a cumulative history of thinking about women's sexual behavior. The questions that persist are those that fit best within the limits permitted by the attachment of available scientific and medical techniques to anxious or hostile heteronormative discourses in the popular media, religion, and psychology.

How persistent are those questions? Robert Spitzer, a professor of psychiatry at Columbia University, claimed in an unpublished study described at the 2001 annual meeting of the American Psychiatric Association that many highly motivated gay and lesbian people can become heterosexual. There followed an avalanche of media attention, in spite of the fact that Spitzer's small sample of two hundred was composed of "ex-gays" referred by antigay religious groups. He interviewed each subject for forty-five minutes. Spitzer (2001) expressed horror at the way "some of the media reported the study as an attempt to show that homosexuality is a choice, and that substantial change is possible for any homosexual who decides to make the effort" (A26).

However, when Spitzer spoke to the *Advocate,* he expressed not only horror but pleasure. "I'm willing to admit that I like controversy and to be in the center of burning debates," he said. To have one's voice heard nationally, to speak with authority on the lives of sexual Others, to say things that can have some effect—good or ill—on the lives of those Others—these are heady rewards gained at small personal cost, won by making a public exhibition of one's loyalty to the conventional terms of the "burning debates" about sexuality.

The history of events like this does not describe an upward curve toward more accurate or humane understanding. Instead the old ideas are recycled, reformulated, and relocated, finding their justification in slightly revised theories and new techniques of investigation and intervention. The research and the discourse it supports succeed as long as they continue to pose, in forms that fit the times and the technologies, the same questions Dörner sought to answer: What induces homosexuality? How can it be prevented or cured? The best response from those who think that nothing good has come from questions like these is not to try to produce more accurate answers to them, but to find ways to resist destructive thinking and coercive practices.

The epigraph from Audre Lorde at the beginning of this section would seem to have no place in the scientific discourses, but it speaks directly to the issues Dörner and so many later researchers have been interested in. Lorde's statement and the body represented there refused to be quarantined as an unholy Other. Lorde spoke of a sexual body able to take up all available roles, a body not rigidly specialized, energized by the desire to make itself again and again, and drawing on all its material possibilities. This is a Babel sort of body, an ambitious cooperative effort. No one agent created its many possibilities. Though it shares in the received categories—submissive and dominant, masculine and feminine—it will not take up a final position on one side or the other, and in doing so, leaves room for "our."

This body differs from the rat/woman hybrid that emerges from Dörner's study in one highly significant way: she is both an agent and a subject. Speaking for herself, she refuses to attribute her sexuality to ultimate or singular causes. Lorde brought the terms "power" and "woman" together in the recognition that they could be joined only "by some aberrant adjective like blind, or hunchback, or crazy, or Black" (Zami, 15). These are terms for hybrid agents who, following Douglas's interpretation of Leviticus, are unclean because they are "imperfect members of their class," or—a truer expression of the same—because they confound "the general scheme of the world" (55). The qualities of such a perverse thinker, speaker, and actor can neither be induced nor prevented by any sovereign agent, because sovereign agents can only act within the boundaries of a world in which all things line up docilely in their given categories.

2
Being Perverse

behold the
great image of authority: a dog's
obey'd in office.
—King Lear

Dizzying heights

The consciousness of heterosexuality as the normal sexual and social identity is crucial to research like Dörner's. Being a "normal heterosexual" has achieved over the course of the last century a marked eminence in the major discourses on sexuality, religion, and social order. The normal heterosexual may not be as interesting as his or her less respectable counterparts, but she turns out to be rare and hard to define. Dörner's implicit definition of normal heterosexuality as the subordination of the passive female to the active male, expressed prototypically in male-dominant sexual intercourse, is familiar but hardly universally accepted, at least when applied to human beings. In any case, I have no plans to try to discover what normal heterosexuality really is. Under the influence of postmodern feminism, I have learned to accept, with apologies to Gertrude Stein, that there is no there there. Normal heterosexuality is most remarkable for what it is not: it is not abnormal. All other sexual behaviors and the identities they are associated with are, to a greater or lesser degree, not normal.

Setting aside as ultimately unanswerable the puzzle of definition leaves me free to consider other (and I believe more fertile) questions: What is the nature of those powers—androgens, the genetic code, God, nature, or common sense—that determine who resides at the pinnacle of sexual value and power? How do people use the hierarchical metaphor, the idea that one can argue meaningfully for the superiority of one sexual identity over another, as a tool for determining status and regulating behavior? What happens to the scofflaws, like radical feminists and sexual perverts, who lack faith in the hierarchical metaphor and put that infidelity into action?

One of the most conventional, and therefore proper, responses to the first question is that God or nature made men and women to reproduce. Therefore, normal heterosexuality is the divinely approved or most natural form of sexual expression, and the best families are composed of a normal heterosexual male/female couple and their biological children. Both normal heterosexuality and the well-functioning nuclear family in which it resides have the singular responsibility for perpetuating, indeed for advancing, the human race.

There are signs of weakness in this conventional response. Among the signs I examine in this chapter are apocalyptic visions of a world spiraling toward the social and sexual chaos that must result from the imminent failure of the family; the marginalization of people who demonstrate a degree of curiosity about or even respect for sexual and social defectors; and, most of all, the relentless need to interpret lives and events to vindicate the hierarchical metaphor in which normal heterosexuality occupies the topmost position.

Paula Gunn Allen (1998), an American Indian, lesbian, and radical feminist scholar, blamed the Anglo-European devotion to religious and social hierarchies for uncontained social plagues including rape and sexual abuse, racist and homophobic violence, the destruction of the environment, genocide, and "all the subtle and gross manifestations of trickle-down conceptualizations of the nature of the good, the real, and the wholesome" (1–2). The sum of these plagues Allen called rape culture. This, the most violent expression of the heterosexual imperative, can be defined most broadly as the material and spiritual degradation of the earth and its people.

Allen recalled talking with a group of New Age practitioners, one of whom pointed upward as she talked about the source of her power to heal others, as if the direction it came from guaranteed its strength and benevolence. Allen found implausible the hierarchical theory of spiritual power the gesture implied. She was convinced that the consequence of perpetuating that theory was a world in which "the oppression and abuse of women is indistinguishable from fundamental Western concepts of social order" (1).

For Allen, the connection between violent oppression and "God the Father" is the "systemic belief that dominance is synonymous with superiority and that superiority is a reflection of the divine" (2). I don't know that Allen is correct in saying that we *believe* that dominance and superiority are necessarily the same thing. It seems to me more likely that people who are in a position to dominate often seek justification by asserting their superiority. Certainly the ability to persuade others of one's moral or spiritual superiority makes it easier to practice dominance, but "higher ups" can often continue to dominate even if their subordinates have no faith in their excellence.

Allen cannot see the women's appeal to God's authority as innocent or benign. Even if their intention is to do good, and even if they, too, feel uncomfortably constrained within hierarchies of power, they are appealing to the divine in order to promote their own mundane ambitions. Whether they believe in God is beside the point, because the reward for using the metaphor effectively is neither truth nor freedom but a better place on the so-called ladder. The idea that power resides on high is integral to how power really works.

Ordinary perverts

Allen's rejection of Father God and patriarchy has everything in common with perversion as it is defined in an influential psychoanalytic interpretation, expressed well by Janine Chasseguet-Smirgel, "The pervert is trying to free himself from the paternal universe and the law. He wants to create a new kind of reality and to dethrone God the Father" (1985, 12). If the male pronoun is replaced by the female, this is an accurate description of Allen's radical feminist project. Perhaps even more curiously, it also reflects the primal myth of the enlightenment, in which the sons overthrow the despotic father to achieve freedom and equality among themselves. Socially rebellious daughters and sons seem to have something in common with sexual perverts: they all refuse to put their faith in the word of accepted authorities.

Chasseguet-Smirgel's best known exemplar of perversion is the Marquis de Sade. Like Allen, the Sadean pervert wants "not to annihilate things but to dissolve and metamorphose them" (4). There is, however, a difference between Allen and Sade that the psychoanalytic model of perversion cannot account for. Whereas Sade wants to usurp the high place of God the Father and rule as a tyrant over a reality of his own making, Allen is convinced that the hierarchy that culminates in God the Father must topple in order to do away with the violence that flourishes in the Sadean fantasy. Sade wants to have God's power to subjugate matter—women in this universe are matter—according to his desire. Allen wants no one to be in a position to subjugate anyone else.

Sade is thought to represent the extreme, but Simone de Beauvoir, for one, accused him of cowardice for only "whipping a few girls," apparently disappointed that he was no more than a middling sadist (17). In fact he terrorized prostitutes and imprisoned young girls hired as domestic servants, beating them and sexually abusing them. Nowhere in writings about Sade is much attention paid to his real-life victims. They were poor, far beneath Sade and de Beauvoir in the class hierarchy. They did not write books. Furthermore, he did not actually kill any of them, and so among those who appreciate the imagination at work in his literary oeuvre, he seemed in practice just an ordinary pervert who either wanted the negative attention or lacked the self-protective faculty that would have motivated him to conceal his unusual sex life.

There is evidence that in some ways Sade really was ordinary. A wealth of research in the 1980s through the early 1990s showed that high percentages of college men had committed sexual assault or admitted they were likely to sexually assault a woman if they thought they would never be found out.[1] A colleague told me recently about a Web site that specializes in amateur photography by men who want to share with other men pornographic pictures of their wives and girlfriends. Over forty thousand of the registered users are military personnel, many of whom contribute a different kind of pornography: photographs of corpses and body parts of Iraqis they have killed.[2]

Men in both examples flout conventional moral authority so that they can assume positions of dominance. Joining together in a brotherhood, they support one another's right to create, own, and share images that represent their ascendance over the bodies of women and over the bodies of dead enemies.

Many men, of course, refuse to join that kind of brotherhood, and some women, once they are in a position to abuse and degrade others, will jump at the chance, as the abuse of Iraqi prisoners at Abu Ghraib illustrates. The discussions of social contract theory and perversion that occupy this chapter will show, however, that gender continues to matter even when we've given up the notion that male and female are polar opposites and analogs for sexual aggressor and passive victim. Nor is it reasonable to dismiss such extralegal cruelties as perversions, outside of and noxious to social order. Allen is right: without sexual and military violence, the world as we know it would not survive.

The hierarchical metaphor

We may protest when we meet up with an institutional obstacle, but we tend to accept without serious questioning that hierarchy is the best and most natural order of individuals, families, institutions, nations, and the cosmos, that domination and subordination are inevitable, and that if the hierarchy fails, political mayhem and psychological bedlam must result.

Using logic similar to Allen's when she deconstructed the myth of power as hierarchy, Michel Foucault wrote, "people accept as truth, as evidence, some themes which have been built up at a certain moment during history, and . . . this so-called evidence can be criticized and destroyed" (1988, 10). One of the themes that concerned Foucault was repression, which Foucault saw not as an essential part of sexual psychology but as a social production, an illusion with material consequences. Believing in repression, we require ourselves to profess certain things about sex and hide the rest—truths, perhaps—in silence or ignorance. He wanted to overthrow the chimera, discredit the supposed evidence, and show people that they are "much freer than they feel" (1988, 10).

If I take the advice implicit in Allen's and Foucault's critiques and try to outwit the hierarchical illusion, the resulting vision strikes me as naïve. Are they really imagining a world so accepting there is no shame and so safe there is no fear? Where no one ever takes advantage of a child's vulnerability and dependence? Where people are so reasonable that they do not mistake dissent for sin?

If so, this is a post-apocalypse far more radical than anything religion ever looked to, a universe so different that I cannot imagine how it would come into being through the unmaking of the world as we know it.

It occurs to me that my skepticism about the better vision is one of the "manifestations of trickle-down conceptualizations of the nature of the good, the real, and the wholesome" to which Allen referred (1). I find it hard to believe that human beings, collectively at least, can be altruistic or farsighted. What I recognize as reality is based on a different idea, that in general human beings will doggedly uphold as precious hollow beliefs they identify as natural or God's will, and that they will tolerate virtually any injury to a designated outsider whose life calls that belief into question. From where I stand, I can see little to suggest that human beings have the collective ability to create a better world. In fact, if we can prevent ourselves from mutual destruction we should be proud of ourselves.

Louis Althusser (1977) wrote, "those who are in ideology believe themselves by definition outside ideology" (13). If he was right, then I should be unable to recognize the origin of my own negative, defeatist perceptions in ideological apparatuses such as family, law, and politics. I should be inhabiting what appears to be a seamless, if cynical, reality, from which flows an endless stream of evidence to confirm my belief that the human capacity for evil is bottomless.

In 1980, Althusser strangled his wife, Hélène Rytman. He later wrote a memoir, published in 1992, in which he tried to explain his actions. Douglas Johnson's introduction to the book implied that Althusser was not a murderer; the strangling was a tragedy, not a crime. Johnson entertained various competing reasons for the tragedy, including Rytman's allegedly controlling nature, a bad reaction to prescription drugs Althusser might have taken, and the possibility that Althusser desired to kill himself but ended up killing his wife instead. Lewis Kirshner, like others who commented on Althusser's life, wasted no sympathy on the victim, but his account was more skeptical of Althusser's various strategies for denying responsibility, including the idea that if the individual subject is "nothing more than a bourgeois illusion, then the man who never existed [i.e., Althusser] could only be a virtual murderer" and the idea that Rytman wanted to be murdered and he was called upon to do the job (230).

In his famous essay on ideology, Althusser twice uses the word "perverse" to describe a man who acts in ways that appear to conflict with his beliefs (127). When that happens, ideology "lends him other ideas corresponding to the actions (however perverse) that he does perform" (127). In the memoir, Althusser announced that he felt silenced and invisible after he killed Rytman. Those feelings were easily accounted for within the ideological framework he used to write off the murder (22). He was rendered silent and invisible because major institutions (familial, judicial, and medical/psychiatric) deprived him of the ability to take responsibility for his own actions. He was called to commit murder by the victim and then hailed as incompetent to stand trial. Like any hapless Althusserian subject, he could not help but respond.

Althusser tried to portray the murder as a kind of healing by suicide: in remarks attributed to an "old doctor friend," Althusser reports that he did Rytman an "immense service" in killing her (282). Althusser ascribed responsibility for his actions to powers far stronger than his (nonexistent) self. It was not he who had and used the power to destroy a life; there was instead a something else (destiny, meaningless chance, a bad childhood, depression, drugs, or "imponderable factors") that determined his actions (285). Whatever that something else was, it could not be held to account, so Althusser was left to deal with consequences.

It is not surprising to find an intelligent murderer manipulating ideas to excuse his crime. Perversion as Althusser used the term is conventional, which is to say that the acts he would consider perverse can be far more easily accommodated under the ruling ideology than can Allen's revolutionary bid to abolish hierarchy. Allen challenged the woman who pointed at the ceiling to identify the source of healing power because that gesture is especially useful for those who want to shuck off responsibility for their violence against or exploitation of others.

Ascribing responsibility for one's actions to a higher source of power is most essentially a plea to be accepted as a member of society. Both the New Age healer who gives credit to a divine source of power outside herself and the murderer who tries to deflect blame onto something or someone else more powerful than himself are performing a common ritual of supplication, asking to have their actions understood and affirmed. Althusser expresses concerns about people who might "cling rigidly to their *personal point of view*" rather than accept his explanations (284; italics in original). But those who don't commit grotesque crimes have similar concerns about whether others will accept their explanations of themselves and their actions. Just about everyone performs manipulations akin to Althusser's. We do it reflexively because this is the price one pays for social acceptance.

We maintain our membership in the world as we know it by working hard to cover the holes so that we don't even have to see them. Freud, whose ideas about the relationship between the individual mind and society I will examine, wrote, "there are countless civilized people who would shrink from murder or incest but who do not deny themselves the satisfaction of their avarice, their aggressive urges or their sexual lusts, and who do not hesitate to injure other people by lies, fraud and calumny, so long as they can remain unpunished for it" (1961, 12). Perhaps being alienated from the community is the most fearful punishment that follows the revelation of one's ordinary, subcriminal evil behavior, but social order as we now think of it only survives because we assimilate some bad practices, most notably hypocrisy. Those most likely to suffer social alienation are not those who satisfy their "aggressive urges" and then deny responsibility or try to avoid detection. It is people like Allen who are most likely to be marked as perverse outsiders. Her overt insistence that we should recognize and demolish ideologies that allow us to rationalize violence violates conventional wisdom, which holds that violence is the sin of the "other."

In every class where my students read Allen, the objection arises that she appeared to advocate what she was criticizing. When Allen wrote, "the only way to transform rape culture is to dismember patriarchal civilization in all of its myriad forms and expressions," we wonder how our entire violence-prone "civilization" could be dismembered without a great deal of violence (1)?

The only radical feminist I know of who carried out a violent act was Valerie Solanas, infamous for her satiric, man-hating *SCUM Manifesto* and for shooting Andy Warhol. Her radical feminist politics are usually credited for the crime, but it seems more likely that her mental instability was the cause. Like Althusser, she spent time in mental hospitals. She also tried to use her own ideas (such as they were) to vindicate herself, but unlike Althusser, she was pleased to take full responsibility for the attempted murder, which she believed was a moral act.

In spite of the gender equality implied by Althusser's and Solanas's notoriety, murder statistics support the argument that men's violence against women vastly outstrips women's violence against men. According to recent U.S. Bureau of Justice statistics, over a third of women who were murdered were killed by a male intimate partner, while less than 4 percent of murders of men were committed by female intimate partners.[3]

The fall

According to Aristotle, "In the first place there must be a union of those who cannot exist without each other; namely, of male and female, . . . and of natural ruler and subject" (*Politics*). What if what must be fails?

The belief that heterosexual marriage and "the family" are falling apart is nearly universal among my students. They tend to hold divorce and women's waged employment responsible for the apparent decline, but many of them come from successful families headed by (mostly female) single parents, and in their experience, the "breakdown of the family" does not mean the end of the world. The more apocalyptic interpretations of changes in family structure are to be found among right-wing Christians, who are particularly alarmed by declining rates of legal marriage, higher rates of single parenthood, any access to abortion, and efforts to secure marriage rights for same-sex couples. Southern Baptists responded to the perceived "tremendous breakdown of family life" by amending their official set of beliefs to emphasize the subordination of women to men's leadership in marriage.[4] If marriage was dissolving as the result of confused gender roles, women's disobedience, and acceptance of homosexuality, then the disorder could be resolved by reasserting that genders are polarized and hierarchically fixed, women are under male authority, and homosexuals are excluded from entering into the marriage contract.

Feminist social contract theorist Carole Pateman (1989) made the clearest argument for viewing the marriage contract as "a political fiction which ceremonially recognizes the patriarchal subjection of a wife and the masculine privileges of a husband," which expresses rather well why the concept of same-sex marriage is even less comprehensible than egalitarian heterosexual marriage to so many (51). Citing Foucault (1979), Pateman argued that civil society depends on "the complicity of subordinates" who believe, erroneously, that they are included in the "fraternal social contract" that guarantees liberty and equality (51). Women are among those who, although disadvantaged in the social contract, are expected to offer their full support to those who are privileged.

The Southern Baptist amendment suggests the gravity of the danger: if wives refuse to "submit graciously," or consent to their own permanent subordination to men, then God will refuse to protect us from the dissolution of society. Out here beyond the Southern Baptist universe, I know only a few heterosexual women of any class or religious background who give even lip service to the idea that wives should be led by their husbands. Furthermore, according to Stephanie Coontz (2005), American men who agree to egalitarian marriages are happier than those who insist on women's subordination (292).[5] However, given both the United States' reputation for being the most sexually conservative among the industrialized nations and the power of the religious right in shaping our social policy and legislation, it is not possible to dismiss what the Southern Baptist Convention says just because its opinions do not coincide with those of people generally.

Pateman focused on contract theorists of the seventeenth and eighteenth centuries, on the premise that modern contract theory evolved from their conceptualizations of the individual, the family, and society. Although Pateman's strict conception of marriage as oppressive of women ignored changes in how women and men think of marriage, at least in some European and American contexts, the implication of her major argument is difficult to refute. Women have ventured far outside the problematic "private sphere" to which contract theorists relegated them, but every step they take is greeted with derisive condemnations of feminists, outcry against the proliferating disorder women are causing, and renewed questions like "are women really fit to succeed in a man's world?" and "who will take care of the children while women are trying to 'fulfill' themselves?"

These arguments about women's place are not much different from those that early contract theorists made. According to Pateman, the subordination of women and their exclusion from the fraternal contract was assumed to ensure order in both the family and the state. Contract theorists expended little effort trying to defend a proposition that seemed self-evident and that was greeted with little resistance.[6] No matter whether women were considered hypothetically equal in strength and ability to men (Thomas Hobbes) or inherently weakened and disordered by their passions (Jean Jacques Rousseau), control over their sexual and reproductive services was at least tacitly understood to be the main issue at stake in the conflicts attending the dawn of organized society. The status of women remained unchanged in democratic (re)origin myths in which "brothers" overthrew the dictatorial father and instituted a social contract for equality and liberty among men. Achieving equality and liberty among men did not require overthrowing hierarchies of power and decision making based on gender, and even Mary Wollstonecraft's thought suffered from what Pateman (1980) described as the dilemma that arises from arguing that citizenship should be gender neutral, but that women's special talents suit them for stay-at-home motherhood (197).

The brothers' agreement about how to guarantee one another fair access to women was later detailed by Sigmund Freud as one of the founding myths of oedipal theory.[7] With Freud, the story about how civilization came to be coincided with the story of the development of the individual and the collective human psyche. One must buy into some version of the fiction—its import if not the literal story—in order to claim a place in civil society, but Freud goes further, assuming that the psychological health of the individual depended on his recreating in his own life the story of the dawn of a version of the liberal state.

According to Freud, women could not fully resolve oedipal conflicts. They lacked the capacity to relive the origin myth, so they would never be fully mature. Pateman acknowledged that women represent a special and difficult class, but her feminist interpretation leads to a very different conclusion: women cannot fully realize the dream of freedom as long as their subordinate status in the sexual contract endures, and it must endure if the contract among brothers is to survive.

Both Foucault and Allen believed that it is possible to rewrite stories like these because they are not accounts of what has been or must be, but social productions subject to revision. Due to the influence of liberal ideals and feminism, marriage has evolved in the United States to accommodate more egalitarian forms than the classical contract theorists, Freud, or evangelical Christianity allowed for, and the legal and social consequences of ending a miserable marriage are less damaging than in previous generations.

Those who have long since abandoned the idea that the good of society depends upon men being able to dictate or override their wives' decisions continue to believe that heterosexuality is the absolute and irreducible basis of human society. Acceptance of that belief is assumed to be the essential kernel of psychological and sexual health in the individual.

From a liberal point of view, a small minority of people can be other than heterosexual without representing a serious threat to social order, as long as everyone accepts the idea that heterosexuality is not just more prevalent, but more essential to human well-being than homosexuality.[8] From a conservative point of view, any departure from a narrowly defined set of heterosexual behaviors and institutions is a dangerous moral failure. But the same heterosexual contract underlies both perspectives. That contract includes not only the elements of gender hierarchy Pateman describes, but an implicit agreement that the ordering principle of heterosexuality, manifest in the male/female couple and their biological children, is all that stands between us and the end of the world.

If one fails to agree, if one somehow eludes some of the regulatory power of heterosexuality, then one is perverse. To be perverse is to promote social, sexual, and reproductive chaos.

All this—perversion as a betrayal of contract, the certainty that "the family" is dissolving, the urgently felt need to protect heterosexual hegemony, anticipation of collective social, spiritual, and psychological chaos—are elements of a system of myths that allow individuals, nations, and religions to justify their own existence and defend their practices.

I began this section with Aristotle's assertion that the relationship of man and woman takes first place, serving as a model for ruler and subject. All such assertions about first and last things are part of the defensive system I just alluded to; they justify the hierarchy that connects origins with ends. Without some idea of an original "state of nature" from which humanity had to emerge, Hobbes (for instance) would have had a hard time justifying our need for a universal social contract. Pointing back to the "state of nature" origin story, and forward to the fearful prospect of humanity's regression if we fail to fulfill our contract, Hobbes suggested methods for suppressing the destructive passions that would lead us back to hell. "As for the passions, of Hate, Lust, Ambition, and Covetousness, [and] what Crimes they are apt to produce, . . . their effects cannot be hindred, but by extraordinary use of Reason, or a constant severity in punishing them" (214–15).[9]

These are the perverse passions. Modern conceptions figure perversion as the union of hate with lust, or equally pertinent, as the denial of sexual and social realities.[10] Unchecked, the passions would turn the individual to crime and the world to bedlam. However, Hobbes is more optimistic about the natural state of man than many. For him, the existence of an organized state demonstrates that man's potential for reason and for order always existed. He is more hopeful than Freud (1933b), who furnished an analogy establishing congruence between structures of the state and the mind: "Our mind, that precious instrument by whose means we maintain ourselves alive, is not [a] peacefully self-contained unity. It is rather to be compared with a modern State in which a mob, eager for enjoyment and destruction, has to be held down forcibly by a prudent superior class" (221).

Attempting to locate the origins of the human psyche and society in the same place, Freud argues that there is a universal mind that can be mapped not only onto the primal events of the oedipal story, but onto current social structures—class divisions, "the modern state," and the family.

Hobbes wrote that cities and kingdoms "are but greater Families" (116), and Freud referred to "the family" as "the germ cell of civilization" (1961, 61).[11] Freud's germ cell grew best in a hierarchical, patriarchal garden. Criticizing communism, he argued that abolishing private property and sexual "prerogative," or a man's right to prevent other men from having sexual access to his wife, would leave humanity with no effective outlet for aggression. It would, therefore, turn on itself. The family would not survive the revolution, and without it, "we cannot . . . easily foresee what new paths the development of civilization could take" (61).

The chain of destruction Freud (1927) fears could only materialize if the structures of the mind were roughly isomorphic with the "modern state" that develops from an original state of savagery and, as the destructive passions suppressed, eventually emerges into civilization. The patriarchal family is the reproductive unit for both the individual and society.[12] If communism succeeded in doing away with it, we would forfeit evolutionary progress.

What is at stake is not just a particular kind of economy or government, but survival itself. Men who can keep down the "masses" in themselves are also likely to be good leaders.[13] Without wise men as leaders, we would not stagnate but regress, returning to a state of nature. For Freud, nature was specifically feminine and relentlessly vicious. If she rules, "She destroys us—coldly, cruelly" (Freud 1964, p. 20). Chasseguet-Smirgel shares with Freud the vision of catastrophe, but she makes nature more the passive victim than the aggressor. The agent of destruction is not communism but the perverse way of thinking, which "makes of our world a Tragic Circus, where the temptation to smooth the Mother-Earth's belly by means of an apocalyptic outburst is becoming more and more insistent" (130). To prevent this from happening, Mother–Earth must be kept pregnant by means of her heterosexual union with reality (the Father). That will help us avoid the end of the world.

Writing about nature at least as reasonably as either Chasseguet-Smirgel or Freud, the Marquis de Sade (1791) recommended adhering to Nature's plan for maintaining a balance that would allow the world to survive. According to Sade, we must have wolves and lambs. Both are essential to Nature's "scheme" to maintain "a perfect equilibrium resulting from the equality of good and evil on earth; the equilibrium essential to the maintenance of the stars, of vegetation and, lacking which, everything would be instantly in ruins" (*Justine*, 609). Sade, naturally, is a wolf.

None of these writers could imagine the survival of a world in which they had no part. Chasseguet-Smirgel, seeing herself as her patients' symbolically fecund mother and wife; Freud, defending a civilization that only survives through the efforts of men like him—patriarchs of the "superior class"; and Sade, figuring himself as the champion of the natural law of predator and prey, all portrayed themselves as crucial to the continuation of human life.

Also crucial is that human life cannot endure without its guardians. The masses, like the id, are defenseless against their own impulses, so the superego, the upper classes, the government, and men as husbands and fathers have the special duty to suppress excess passions, their own and those of their subordinates and dependents.[14] So profound is the threat that civilized people keep themselves from knowing what their wishes are: "If we were to know them we should be appalled, alike by their subject-matter, their unrestraint and indeed the mere possibility of their existence" (Freud 1933b, 222). We may even construct imaginary memories as part of our defense system, "just as every nation disguises its forgotten prehistory by constructing legends" (1966, 368). Presumably those who have the most responsibility for maintaining order must, like Freud, know somewhat more about our unconscious wishes than the rest of us do in order to perform the duties that keep us from destroying civilization. Without that pressure from above, aggression unchanneled and desire unrepressed would bring us all down, individually and collectively.

The stories I've been examining, including Freud's, vindicate the rule of the strong—the morally superior, or the more rational, or simply the more vicious—over the weak. It seems that Freud was right: we produce elaborate myths to justify our sense of our own importance and conceal, even from ourselves, our baser wishes. In this sense, there is not much difference between Freud's or Sade's catastrophic fantasies and the apocalyptic visions, promoted primarily by fundamentalist Christians, of a world demolished by liberal tolerance of abortion, heterosexual promiscuity, feminism, and homosexuality. The Christians point up to God, Sade to nature, and Freud to science (and psychoanalysts to Freud) as the source of wisdom, but no matter whose authority they believe they are channeling, they take on themselves special responsibility for saving the rest of us from ourselves.

Terrifying New Worlds

Repressive clinical, religious, and legal approaches to perversion are often justified by means of the same unexamined hierarchical metaphor. Here Freud's idea that fantasy and reality may become mixed up in convoluted ways applies particularly well. In modern thought, sexual perversion is the union of hate with lust, the conjoined sin most liable to result in criminal sexual behavior. Sexual perversion figures as one of many threats to those who imagine themselves high on the ladder of social and sexual value and, therefore, as crucial to the maintenance of civilization. In their psychological reality, almost anything—any identity, behavior, belief, or desire—that appears to flout authority can be read as perverse. For them, homosexuality is a particularly dangerous perversion wherever it erupts into social activism, refusing to accept being set apart (and down) from the highest social institutions: heterosexuality, marriage, and "the family." When the so-called perverts refuse to occupy a low and isolated place, they are repudiating the fantasies of those whose self-concept rests on seeing themselves as defenders of an embattled civilization. In fact, however, such fantasies require enemies who can be feared and opposed, but never fully vanquished. Gay activists fit the bill at least as well as skulking homosexuals. Having no enemy to defend against would be far worse, almost as frightening as having nothing that needs defending.

Perversion is defined and managed institutionally, but according to modern psychology, it originates in a very private place: childhood, in a failed family. Christian conservatives have at least one thing in common with Freud and Hobbes: they believe there is a causal connection between the form and function of the family and that of the state. For them, being religious and believing in the singular sacredness of the nuclear heterosexual family place one high on the moral hierarchy. For them, Christianity and "the family" make everything possible: a healthy mind, positive life experience, spirituality, good government, and society itself. If the Christian, heterosexual nuclear family fails to replicate itself, that is a calamity that must reverberate throughout the larger systems, creating distortions and functional failures everywhere. Unless we can be protected against, in particular, the perverting effects of feminism and homosexuality, the family and therefore the nation will no longer exist. As James Dobson (2001), president of the right-wing organization Focus on the Family, described the problem, "the forces arrayed against the family are almost irresistible. Homosexual activists, radical feminists, abortion zealots and haters of Christianity have banded together to bring down the old order and substitute their own version of the *Brave New World*."

When Allen recommended dismantling the "philosophical and social order" in order to bring about a world free of violence, she was indeed recommending the end of the world in which thoughts like Dobson's are intelligible. According to Allen, we can make another, better world "by way of a passionate, thoroughgoing" commitment to "polyarchy and equality" that is based on "a secure, articulate, formal sense of the Feminine" (13–14). This would be a world without centralized governments. Authority and responsibility for communities would devolve on many. I doubt that an abstract or embodied feminine is an ideal replacement for the conventional masculine deity, but the main idea is clear enough: no one should subjugate another person to his or her will at all, let alone in the name of God. In order to bring this happier world into being, we would have to let go of the expectation that philosophy, religion, language, and culture ought to achieve a unified whole, and we would have to let go of the idea that power comes from above. From the Christian perspective, this is the equivalent of atheism, but God's existence or quantity are not in question here. Instead, the focus is on real-world events that demonstrate the marked tendency of monotheists to use coercive or violent means to impose their self-serving concept of "oneness" on everyone.

Allen was right that religious, sexual, social, and class hierarchies, far from keeping our worst passions at bay, are the perfect environment for cultivating them. For that reason alone, I was ready to dismiss Allen's brave new world as hopelessly utopian almost before she drew its rough outlines. I can see no way to progress toward the commitments she believes would make the new world possible. I found nothing in Allen or Foucault to suggest how we can overcome the human defects that create the world as we know it. Even those who don't actually wish death or misfortune on others must, I believe, exert every ounce of will, reason, and empathy they possess to avoid behaving in selfish, irrational, shortsighted, uncaring, intolerant, aggressive, and jealous ways.

Reality as metaphor

Like any healing discipline, including the New Age versions Allen encountered, psychoanalysis is supposed to intervene in a dysfunctional life and set it back on the right course. The power, the source of suffering or cure, is immune to ordinary observation, concealed in divine ascendance, molecular tininess, labyrinthine wisdom, or the unconscious. Intervention means deciphering evidence from the sufferer's life, fantasies, and dreams, with reference to an arcane code that derives from that abstract source of power.

For psychoanalysts, Freud is the ultimate interpreter, but he could do nothing without theoretical intangibles such as the id/ego/superego structure of the mind, the unconscious (so much of which is conscious for the properly trained psychoanalyst), and primal scenes. The latter are experienced both personally and collectively, but they need not be remembered nor even have occurred to have the power to direct our psychological and social development. These unverified events unfold within us, where—uncontrolled, misunderstood, or diverted from their proper plan—they disrupt the body and mind. No doubt my own lack of faith in collective human wisdom and goodness could be explained with reference to this interpretive system, but as the "sufferer" I am not qualified to make that attempt except, perhaps, under the guidance of a psychoanalyst.

This is what makes the interpreter essential to the process of healing. She or he is the real-world conduit through which power from above (or beyond) heals those who suffer and punishes those who generate social disorder.

A skeptical or perverse eye like mine sees this hierarchical arrangement as a perfect setup for abuse. We—those who are in need of interpretive help and healing intervention—are supposed to be looking up toward something of amazing power and beauty that is beyond our reach and perhaps beyond our comprehension. While we are looking up, the essential action is happening down here, in the relations between people. The misdirection benefits those who convince themselves and others that they have gained special access to some higher power and can deliver its messages to those who lack such direct access—those of us down below. As long as the mediator points upward, directing attention toward the metaphorical source of power, she or he makes it harder to see that power is produced where the interpreter/healer and the sufferer meet. Our acceptance of the hierarchical illusion allows those who have higher institutional status, or can claim a more direct link to some ultimate source of power, to entertain no truth that disadvantages them.

Major institutions—judicial/penal, educational, medical, and religious—generate meanings for dissent, suffering, or deviations from accepted behavior that, above all, allow the institutional hierarchy to continue to exist. Those of us who work inside major institutions or who are affected by decisions made there (i.e., everyone) can debate as long as we like about who has cornered the truth, but few question whether the power to know, and therefore the power to decide, really does derive from a free and higher source: God, Reason, Nature, The People.

Anyone who behaves as though some such source does not exist may be marked as childish, a perverse Peter Pan who thinks he can violate natural law and get away with it. Like Althusser, judged to have murdered his wife while temporarily insane, the pervert lacks responsibility and therefore authority. He can appear as a sinner, rebel, victim, or vicious criminal. In psychoanalysis, he is most likely to be portrayed as trapped in psychological infancy, subject to deep psychosexual distortions, his bizarre behaviors beyond his control.

In psychoanalysis there are two extremes of the family, one that represents the pinnacle of healthy, normal heterosexuality and another that breeds perversion. The two families represent heaven and hell, life and death, fertility and barrenness respectively. Their reality is more metaphysical than material. At the center of the family, no matter which, the male/female reproductive pair and the primal scenes they enact are enshrined as the original and ultimate source of virtually all satisfaction and suffering.

Juan Pablo Jiménez described from a psychoanalytic perspective the internal world of perversion. He wrote that for the pervert "the parental couple and, with it, sexuality, are felt to be empty, non-generative and misleading" (2002, 76). For Jiménez, anyone who does not believe that the parental couple is the living center of sexual and reproductive life is perverse, and therefore, dysfunctional.

The pain Jiménez's patients live with and the harm they do to others are real. Their perversions originate in lived experience and have material effects. But that reality takes second place in Jiménez's account to the relationship between the psychoanalyst and his idealized vision of the heterosexual couple and its progeny. Jiménez pays homage to what Deleuze and Guattari referred to as "daddymommyme," the dominance of the heterosexual reproductive unit over every psychological and political experience. Their alternative metaphor for the production of desire, the system of desiring machines, provides for a more dispersed production of desire than the parental couple permits, but it is their recognition that "sovereign Oedipus" does not merit his position on high that appeals most to my argument (54). Granting such power to any single developmental concept, assuming its preeminence and universality, allows one person (the psychoanalyst) to associate himself with a sovereign power (the psychoanalytic mind via its first revealer, Freud), to believe he is its agent, and to trust that those who suffer or create disorder (perverts) could be set right if they could assimilate the wisdom he conveys.

Even in the hands of an authority who intends to do good, paternalism like this is destructive. It impoverishes and distorts interpretations of the material of patients' lives because the person in authority only acknowledges the limited evidence that he can use to sustain his relationship with the sovereign power.

A de-paternalized authority would give up the hierarchical illusion, base his claim to authority on factors closer to home, and, most painfully, enact more horizontal relations of kinship with the other. In the next chapter, I use the hopeful example set by Robert Stoller to show how abandoning paternal authority can improve theory and the interpretation of evidence.

Jiménez's exploration of the territory where his reality and that of his patient overlap is reflective and intelligent, but when he stands on the boundary, trying to observe what is taking place beyond the limits of what they can agree on, he invalidates the patient and loses the opportunity to stand apart from his interpretations in order to gauge their accuracy. According to Jiménez, the pervert inhabits "a pseudo-reality, a world of delusion where the experiences of castration, the experience of the differences between human beings and the diversity of realities that makes the world we speak of precisely a human world do not exist" (68).

The pervert may well occupy a dangerous pseudoreality, but failing to oedipalize one's experience is hardly a measure of one's madness. As the healing professional, Jiménez, in contrast to his perverse patient, assigns himself and the oedipal myth to the real, human reality that is available only to those who have accepted the psychoanalytic meaning of the difference between men and women. Perverse perspectives have no place in the precisely human world Jiménez knows.

And yet, the psychoanalyst is more vulnerable than most to the effects of perversion because his profession takes him so close to the boundary between the normal and the perverse. In contact with the erotic world of his patient, Jiménez writes, "perversion appears in the analyst's mind like a surreptitious and surprising transgression of the basic agreement that makes possible and provides a structure for intersubjective encounter, extending even to the alteration of the rules of Aristotelian logic" (71). Jiménez faced a choice: he could fall victim to the "siren call" of the pervert's pseudoreality and remain immobilized in a symbolically homosexual relation, or he could analyze the perversion indirectly, "from its 'periphery'" (71).

Like a good psychoanalytic witness, Jiménez secured his position by allying himself with sovereign Oedipus, who endowed him with the power to bring the perversion out of its "really internal" hiding place and into the light of "shared reality" (67).[15] It was Oedipus that preserved Jiménez from the seductive disruptions of logic that perversion represents and reaffirmed his position in the nonperverse, heterosexual real world.

The stakes are high. Whoever heeds the siren call of perversion faces the prospect of losing professional authority, of finding himself merged with the person on the recumbent side of the analytic contract. More poignantly, the choice lies between membership in the human family and the "despair" of isolation from that family (69). No wonder that Chasseguet-Smirgel, who had a great deal of trouble convincing her angry, aggressive patient Romaine that his fantasies, preoccupations, and dream images showed "that it was the sexual activity of his parents as a couple . . . that was at stake," pressed on despite his denials (125). Heterosexuality, symbolized in the reproductive parental couple and its oedipal consequences, is the social and psychological forebear of the analytic method, which in its turn produces the crucial distinction between the psychoanalyst and the patient (70). Psychoanalytic training institutes have been reluctant to admit gay students and, when they do allow them to undergo training, have often declined to authorize them to practice. Homosexuality is suspect because it implies reluctance to agree fully to the social, biological, psychological reality of heterosexual primacy. That agreement makes one a healthy adult.

I could maintain membership in the human family while denying faith in Freudianism.[16] But what happens if I say that heterosexuality might not, after all, be the bedrock, the basic human sexual mode that organizes our minds and societies? If psychoanalysis's stock has fallen, it is because it makes heterosexuality, in the form of "sexual difference" and "the parental couple," the central fact around which all meaning collects. When I proposed this to psychoanalytically inclined colleagues, their reactions ranged from angry outrage to embarrassment on my behalf. How could I come up with such ridiculous ideas?

Hoping to distinguish radical doubt from a diagnosable condition (and hold on to membership in the human family), I only side with the perverts theoretically. Fortunately, Jiménez and I may not be so far apart after all. Jiménez left some room for the proposition that the distinction between perverse and nonperverse positions is permeable when he said that perverts subvert "the (alleged) truth of the vitality of the parental coitus" (72). A truth alleged is not proven, and yet, as a "'sharable' fantasy" it is the basis of what Jiménez describes as "*the psychic reality that we assume is shared by our fellows*" (67; italics in original). Chasseguet-Smirgel, less willing than

Jiménez to acknowledge the propositional status of reality, cites a story in which a living nightingale and her song (representing what is "true") are displaced in people's affections by a glittery robotic substitute (representing what is "false" and therefore perverse). The "living" nightingale is a figure in a story, no more real than the fake that takes its place, but Chasseguet-Smirgel does not bring this insight into her analysis (1985, pp. 66–67).

There are some metaphors you are not supposed to recognize as such because, once you set ignorance aside, you are like Eve eating the fruit: you end up knowing far too much. Knowing too much means realizing that the eating of the fruit is an element in a didactic story about the consequences of disobedience to a supreme authority. If you have eaten, however, you know that authority is something other and more proximate than the story says it is, that the power to do good doesn't come from above, nor does evil come from below, but all that is produced in the creation of hierarchical relations between people. Knowing too much is a disobedience so bad that you cannot be allowed to remain in Eden, but it doesn't matter any longer because the dread of expulsion cannot hold you once you have acknowledged that it too is a metaphor, just another way of representing what has already happened the moment you can no longer affirm that Adam's union with Eve is the seed from which all meaning grows.

In this figural universe, anything can be exchanged for anything else, and that is Chasseguet-Smirgel's definition of perversion. "It is as if the equation penis = child = faeces, established by Freud (1917), should be taken literally" (91). This specious equation results from an unsuccessful oedipal conflict. The boy should project "his Ego Ideal onto his father" so that he can aspire to take the father's place someday with someone like his mother. The implication is that healthy, nonperverse people accept the oedipal conflict as literally true even though it, like the perverse alternatives, is laced with fantasies, projections, and metaphors.

Perverts like Sade, lacking faith in what usually passes for reality, cook up another pseudoreality of which they are master. The reality they are (really) out of touch with is nothing like the truth bird in Chasseguet-Smirgel's story. The reality they are out of touch with is that women are real, not mere matter for the pervert/god to play with in his figural universe.

It is much harder to recognize that kind of truth than it is to accept the old stories as true, but the distinction between reality and "as if" is crucial because it describes the difference between Sade and Allen, between those who advocate inflicting rage on the bodies of others and those who refuse to abandon the ideal of a nonviolent world.

Sharing a fantasy

Those who lack faith can seek evidence, but I have encountered no convincing evidence that heterosexuality, or any other sexual orientation, represents alpha and omega of social, sexual, and psychological functioning. The painful lives of Jiménez's patients demonstrate how much distress and disorder can attend heterosexual practice, but observing people under ordinary circumstances is not much more reassuring. When I consider the conventionally heterosexual women I have known who describe their relationships with men in terms very much like those attributed to the pervert, as empty of the security and satisfaction that they had believed should reside there, it seems unlikely that the pervert's disillusionment suffices to distinguish her from her nonperverse counterpart.

With that recognition, what I see begins to diverge so far from Jiménez's views that he might well consider me perverse.

Jiménez's pervert is essential to maintaining the psychoanalyst's world. His pervert may seem to thumb his nose at institutional authority, but by definition the pervert is under the dominion of the authority who names his disorder. If the pervert could get away, s/he would be something else altogether, something inconceivable in psychoanalysis: a being not subject to oedipal interpretation. Lacking a pervert (or at least a neurotic) to analyze, the psychoanalyst would have two alternatives. The first is that he could give up on the psychoanalytic system, which in any case would only allow him to occupy an authoritative position as long as he believed in the universal applicability of Oedipus. If he abdicated, he would share the pervert's apparent fate, having lost faith in the parental couple and its oedipal progeny.

To avoid reaching that point, however, he could salvage the therapeutic relation by taking up both positions, analyst and patient, as Helene Deutsch and Joan Riviere did in their case studies. In that way he would preserve the belief system that supports his membership in the human family and the psychoanalytic fraternity. As long as he didn't think too hard about the dynamics of transference and countertransference when the patient is so intimately an aspect of the self, he could continue to interact with the system and its hierarchies as if they were intact and functioning.

There is no reason to think that Jiménez constructed the illusion like those of Deutsch and Riviere. Instead, because of his empathy and concern for his patient, he admits working hard not to be seduced into identifying with the pervert's desire. At the same time, he seeks to reorient their mutual identification by inducing the pervert to join in the shared fantasy of the parental couple. For Jiménez, the most ideal outcome would eradicate the pervert and leave behind a self ready to believe in the fecundity of the parental couple.

It would be unconscionable to undermine this shared fantasy if believing in it had the effect of bringing an end to sexual abuse of children, harassment, stalking, and rape, all criminal behaviors typically associated with sexual perversion. If, as psychoanalysis generally maintains, perversion is the union of hostility and lust, then only coercive or violent sexual behaviors should be considered perverse. There is no evidence that a belief in the moral primacy of reproductive heterosexuality reduces sexual violence. There is, however, some evidence that rapists are likely to judge many sexual acts negatively: "Even heterosexual acts other than genital intercourse may be regarded as 'perverted,' and masturbation, likewise, may be thought of as abnormal" (Birnbaum 1979, 29). Clearly, however, they did not perceive sexual violence toward women as perverse.

Robert Altemeyer, probably the most dedicated and prolific researcher of "right wing authoritarianism" (RWA) cited other researchers' studies showing that men who score high on his RWA scale are more likely to experience "sex guilt" (1996, 28). They are also more likely to be hostile toward women and to have committed sexual assault, but whether rape strikes them as a more perverse or shameful act than masturbation is an unanswered question (1996, 28). Altemeyer's own studies yielded different results; he found that all his undergraduate male subjects, no matter how they scored on the right-wing authoritarianism scale, were remarkably (and from a woman's point of view, chillingly) "likely to attack and manipulate women" to obtain sex (189).[17]

Altemeyer suggested that his results meant that men "often do not think with their brains" (189). I disagree. What the results show is that when it serves their interests, men of all political stripes are likely to adopt an authoritarian, or perhaps utilitarian, attitude toward women. The men who believe that the Bill of Rights applies to everyone are as likely to have coerced women sexually as the men who would be glad to see it repealed or honored only for people who share their views (1992, 115).

Altemeyer's findings lend support to the studies I cited earlier regarding the number of rapes college men commit and the willingness of many to commit rape if they thought they would not be found out and punished. However, most of the men Altemeyer surveyed did not use physical force;

instead, they applied "continual arguments and pressure" until a woman gave in (1996, 183). "Giving in" means giving consent (even if begrudgingly or because one cannot see a way to refuse), so these men broke no laws. They cannot be considered perverse, either. At least among the men Altemeyer surveyed, acting coercively toward a woman is no less normal than backing down respectfully when a woman says no, and attempting rape is not an unusually aggressive strategy either. What all this means is that Allen's indictment of "rape culture" is anything but groundless.

The signs of perversion in Sade, therefore, were not his manipulative tactics or his violence toward women, but that his writings celebrated the prohibited mixings whose significance Mary Douglas illuminated in Purity and Danger. If Sade had raped women quietly, as other men of his class did, and as a substantial minority of modern college men have said they would, his behavior would have been tolerated, especially since his victims were mostly poor women unguarded by other men.

As Patemen observes, Sade was an innovator in favoring contract over status, a strategy that has helped consolidate "the modern form" of patriarchy that overlooks social and economic differences between men and women in matters of law (1988, 187). In Sade's day, women's social and legal status meant that they entered into sexual contracts with men not as free and equal individuals, but as subordinates before the fact. Even the woman who trounced Sade so effectively, Marie-Madeleine de Montreuil, his once-fond mother-in-law, enjoyed her power to influence events not because that privilege belonged rightfully to her but because her husband was, according to Francine du Plessix Gray, "a self-effacing Milquetoast" (49). This derogatory term, together with du Plessix Gray's half-admiring, half-condemning portrayal of "la Présidente" de Montreuil, reinforces the impression that there is something distasteful about the union of an unassuming husband to an aggressive wife. In effect, neither partner met the terms of the marriage contract, which requires that a woman submit graciously to a man's leadership. The marriage of the Marquis de Sade to de Montreuil's daughter was, in that sense at least, closer to the traditional ideal; for many years, she seems to have obeyed her husband's every decree, no matter how bizarre or humiliating.

The images of women Sade purveyed occupy the same magic category as Chasseguet-Smirgel's real nightingale. They are fictional devices whose promise of pleasure survives only as long as we agree that they represent some higher truth.

I read some of Pauline Réage's *The Story of O* when it made the rounds among my friends in high school.[18] It was supposed to be revolutionary because a woman wrote it, but I could not feel its appeal. Probably I was not the only one who suspected there was something fishy about the proposition that the best a woman could do, given the choice, was to leave all her decisions to others. I have since heard passionate defenses of O that cling precisely to this idea: the woman *chose* to give her entire self up to love, and so her fate (in the end she kills herself) was a triumph. Like Sade's wife, "O" agreed to every mortification. She signed the contract freely, and could have walked away from beatings (etc.) any time, but she found spiritual and erotic fulfillment in subjection and eventual annihilation.

Sade has been attractive to certain feminist (or quasi-feminist) scholars and writers, including Jane Gallop, Francine Du Plessix Gray, Jessica Benjamin, Angela Carter, and Simone de Beauvoir. Some have argued that in his female characters, Sade captured something authentic, the spirit of women who taunt or otherwise compel men's sexual compliance, or of women capable of performing without remorse the cruelest acts of violence, or who give their consent to be coerced because they like the helplessness, the freedom from self, they experience when a man controls and hurts them. The question is whether these characterizations of women resonate because they reflect something authentic about women or because they are familiar to anyone who consumes literature, myth, or movies.

For me, however, reading the novel was like a trip to the dentist. I was bored, numb, and uncomfortable. I didn't finish it. As a newly minted woman, shouldn't I have felt at least some affinity with "O"? If "O" was a revelation, a radical, true vision of woman's erotic desire, then what was I?

What I was up against was this: what women think and feel in reality is varied, changeable, and mutable. Reality cannot compete with the appeal of an evocative and symmetrically satisfying metaphor. When Jessica Benjamin (1988) turned her attention to *The Story of O*, she embedded her discussion in a tradition of psychoanalytic theory that assumes that women in general—real women, not concepts of femininity or characters in novels—share the tendency to certain kinds of psychological pathology. The idea is that masochistic desire and its obligatory effacement are normal for women. In her analysis of the character of O, Benjamin suggested that the willingness of O to submit to "oppression, humiliation, and subservience" represented people's "complicity with their own deepest desires" (55). She wrote, "O's great longing is to be known, and in this respect she is like any lover, for the secret of love is to be known as oneself . . . However, this knowing can only go so far, because there is progressively less of O the subject left to be known" (60). The metaphor of O slips into the posited reality of "any lover," whose great but unrealizable longing is to be known through the experience of being oppressed, humiliated, and subservient. Benjamin didn't analyze any male characters who longed to be known in this or any other way, so the lovers out here in the uncertain land of the real who cannot satisfy their desire to be known must be female. All this suggests what I lacked as a reader of O: I lacked the ability to appreciate that the page-by-page unraveling of O was the revelation of the great secret of heterosexual love: that women long to be known by men, or failing that, to be exterminated.

Benjamin noted that "the actual practice of sadomasochism frequently reverses heterosexual patterns" and "is just as likely to occur in homosexual relationships," but she doesn't have to analyze any of these alternatives, because they imitate heterosexual patterns of male dominance and female submission. That is the model the rest of us must follow, for better or for worse.

What can be known, by readers or lovers, about woman as O is that she is nothing but the metaphoric proposition that "woman is a cipher." For a psychoanalytic theorist and for fans of the novel, that proposition must seem at once elegant and tragically romantic. For someone like me (i.e., someone perversely unmoved by the revelation of the great secret), what O connotes is not women's "complicity with their own deepest desires," but the complicity of a dead-end proposition about the nature of femininity with the conventions of heterosexuality. O represents the venerable idea that woman, lacking a penis, also lacks a fully developed self and must try to get one by getting a man to love her. To really love a woman, then, a man would first have to believe that he had the power to endow her with a self (his own), or to deny her that privilege.

This idea flatters neither sex, but it represents the kind of thinking that allowed Benjamin to argue that "if a woman has no desire of her own, she must rely on that of a man, with potentially disastrous consequences for her psychic life" (89). What Benjamin did not say was that the consequences are even more disastrous if the man's own sense of self is so feeble that he cooperates in the woman's desire to be exterminated, as was the case in *The Story of O.*

But even that "woman's desire" isn't hers. There can be neither pleasure nor pain where there is no one to feel it. The romantic sentiments that attach to the image of the selfless woman in love are no more revolutionary than the similarly conventional assumptions about the selfless mother or the general feminine incapacity that Pateman identified as underpinning the "sexual contract." *The Story of O* was not a revelation of the radical possibilities of female erotic desire but a logical literary consequence of failing to think of women as being there.

The privilege of naïveté

Even Michel Foucault, who tried to dismantle the imaginary structures that maintain some of men's positions of authority over men, was no more willing than Sade (or Réage, or Benjamin) to take seriously the consequences of assuming male prerogative and female submission and theoretical nonexistence. The subject in the case Foucault addressed was a nineteenth-century vagrant farmworker, a "simple-minded" man who sought "a few caresses from a little girl, just as he had done before and seen done by the village urchins round about him" (*History*, 31).

As Foucault told the story, the man was simply following the lead of his much younger fellows by seeking sexual gratification from a girl who should be willing to grant such favors. Foucault represents the event as "an everyday occurrence in the life of village sexuality," and no doubt he is essentially correct: it is not unusual, even now, for men to expect little girls to satisfy their sexual desires (31). The girl's parents, however, complained to the authorities, and the farmworker eventually ended up incarcerated in a hospital. What Foucault finds most relevant about the story is "the pettiness of it all," the way that various regulatory institutions collaborate to punish the man for seeking these "inconsequential bucolic pleasures" from the little girl (31).

The pleasures Foucault refers to, like his entire account of the case, focus on the man and his needs. However, it is hardly necessary to have actually been a little girl to know that being accosted by a homeless derelict who wants you to touch his penis is far more likely to produce feelings of fear and disgust than a happy willingness to cooperate.

This problem is crucial to the questions about power Foucault was attempting to pursue, but he did not consider the girl at all. For Foucault, as for the farmhand, the little girl is a cipher, an "O." He expressed disgust that the farmhand fared so badly in the "whole machinery for speechifying, analyzing, and investigating" to which he was subjected, but I am more concerned about how difficult it is, given the paucity of information

Foucault offers, even to pose questions about the girl. What happens in the life of a girl who, caught up in the ubiquitous machinery of sex and gender, has virtually no space to consider her own needs? Were her parents seeking to protect her when they reported him, or did they consider her to be sullied? When the man was taken into custody, did she feel relieved or did she—like many victims of sexual abuse—feel guilty? How might the conflict between being expected to be a sexless innocent and yet being expected to perform "sexual favors" for men on demand affect her sexual life?

Foucault's lack of interest in how being subject to various, and conflicting, disciplinary powers might affect the girl was due ultimately to a loophole in his concept of power. Power, Foucault said, "is a total structure of actions brought to bear upon possible actions; it incites, it induces, it seduces, it makes easier or more difficult; . . . it is nevertheless always a way of acting upon an acting subject" (Subject, 220).

Representing power as its own agent is a mystification akin to pointing at the ceiling. It encourages one to forget that the total structure Foucault referred to is comprised of people (i.e., acting subjects). The farmhand was not only acted upon by power; he also acted upon the little girl, based on his expectation that she should give him sexual satisfaction. We do not learn what the girl did—give in? resist vocally? struggle physically? complain later to her parents?—but she was as much an acting subject as the farmhand. The other crucial player was Foucault, the voice of the story. Foucault was positioned to make choices about whose interests he would advocate and whose he would forget. Foucault's choice not to represent the girl as at least a potential subject caught up in the "total structure" of power was part of the mystification. She had to be discounted so that the farmhand could take the part of an innocent being persecuted for nothing.

Altemeyer summed up the data on sexual violence he collected from surveys of female students by asking the reader to imagine any group of eight women seated near one another in a classroom. His data showed that seven of those women had been sexually harassed, two had successfully defended themselves against a rapist, one was raped, and one was sexually abused as a child (1996, 186). Altemeyer was "staggered" by the range of potential child abusers—in the twenty-first century there are plenty of stand-ins for Foucault's farmhand—but the most common assailants were fathers and uncles.

Freud, more inclined than many to delve into questions about women's sexuality, wrote that although sometimes girls really have been "seduced" by peers or adults, many such memories are false, the result of complex unconscious machinations. "If a girl tells you she was raped in her childhood, by her father, there can be no doubt either of the imaginary nature of the accusation or of the motive that has led to it" ("Paths," 370). This was the essential story on which Freud based his ideas about female sexuality and feminine personality: girls unconsciously want to have sex with their fathers. The girls project the tabooed desire onto its innocent object, the father who then stands accused of terrible, but imaginary, crimes. The hapless father, therefore, has a good deal in common with the farmhand.

Before this revelation, Freud had believed for a while that he had found the singular root of his patients' hysteria in perverse sexual practices adults (primarily men) inflicted on them when they were infants and toddlers.[19] However, Freud had a hard time convincing some of his patients they had been abused. After confronting one of his patients with his conviction that she had been "seduced" by her father, Freud was disappointed when she took matters into her own hands:

> When I thrust the explanation at her, she was at first won over; then she committed the folly of questioning the old man himself [her father], who . . . swore a holy oath as to his innocence.
>
> She is now in the throes of the most vehement resistance . . . . I have threatened to send her away and in the process convinced myself that she has already gained a good deal of certainty which she is reluctant to acknowledge. (Freud 1985, 220–21)[20]

It was easy for Foucault to forget about the little girl because she could not confront him with his errors, but in his female patients, Freud was dealing with women who could assert their own interests and investigate their own lives. Eventually, Freud decided he was wrong about women, but not because he began to trust what they said about themselves. Instead, Freud replaced his first founding truth of women's sexuality (that they deny paternal abuse) with another (that they deny desiring their fathers). Replacing abuse-denial with desire-denial made for a theoretical earthquake, but the relationship of Freud to his subject did not change: he remained steadfast on the shifting ground of his patients' unreliable memory (1917, 367).

Allen Esterson (1998) demonstrates convincingly that Freud's about-face resulted not from a revelation of truth but from an urgent desire to come up with a more winning theory. In the theoretical universe Freud developed, the feminine unconscious was structured around the wish to take the mother's place in the parental couple. Freud seems to have reworked the scanty evidence he had assembled in support of the "seduction" theory to support a competing oedipal theory of female sexuality, and along the way developed "the procedure that Freud was soon to describe as 'psychoanalysis'" (4).

One must swallow the notion that girls' budding (but unconscious) sexual desires tend to gather more or less universally around their fathers in order to believe the rest of the story. In that story, the analyst's archaeological probing exposes unconscious fantasies of traumatic paternal "seduction," fantasies that the girl uses to absolve herself of her forbidden, equally unconscious, father-desire.[21] (Underlying father-desire was a far more infantile mother-desire that, as we will see, could lead a woman down a dead-end homosexual path, but Freud was more interested in fathers and daughters.) Psychoanalysts faithful to Freud's ideas assume that a woman patient will typically resist admitting her desire for her father which, after all, she is not aware she has. A woman can admit, deny, accuse, or be indifferent to the proposal: any response corroborates the theory, which describes psychological events that occurred in the past and need not be actually recalled. Fragments of memory, dreams, or imaginings provide the evidence, and it requires analytic pressure and heavy interpretive assistance to gather enough evidence to support the basic assumption.

If the account were true, then female sexuality would have its roots in a perverse (but heterosexual) desire. The girl's desire for her father is perverse because it involves both hatred (for the mother, later for the father) and lust. Thus perversion is the forerunner of normal heterosexuality. We have achieved normal heterosexuality when we accept the "parental couple" as ideal to be preserved and emulated. At that point, we have largely overcome the hatred and lust that characterizes the earlier period.

This explains why both perverse and nonperverse sexualities are supposed to derive their energy from an idea of heterosexual coupling. The significant distinction is that nonperverts internalize the male/female parental couple, which they have constructed through oedipal processes. They grant that coupling elevated status, no doubt both consciously and unconsciously. People suffering from perversions, by contrast, refuse to recognize heterosexuality as the model of sexual probity and decline the social/sexual contract (the shared "reality") the parental couple represents.

If Jiménez was right, however, perverts obsessively reenact the traumatic revelation of the so-called heterosexual lie in their own sexual practice. Far from escaping, they carry the dead (but revivable) remains of the parental couple everywhere with them.

At this point it makes sense to distinguish between perversion and skepticism. My reading of Freud and Jiménez is skeptical, meaning that for me the parental couple represents neither a universal ordering principle nor death and meaninglessness, but is, like the nightingale Chasseguet-Smirgel invokes, an imaginary entity that gives the analyst greater scope to interpret what patients say as evidence in support of a universal theory of human psychology.

Skepticism urges me to doubt that Jiménez was correct in saying that the paternal sexual abuse one of Jiménez's patients suffered as a child was significant because it interfered with his ability to internalize the idea that the parental couple is the vital source of being. It seems more likely that such abuse would do the most damage in the patient's immediate and material world. The son might find himself unable to trust his father, future sexual partners of either sex, and/or his own sexual responses. In the worst outcome, he might replicate his father's crimes. Or he might be resilient enough to quarantine the trauma, assign responsibility to the father who abused him, and move on to healthier relationships. There is no need to invoke the parental couple, dead or alive, to understand this much.

It is important to distinguish between losing trust in a real person—oneself or one's father, for instance—and losing trust in an idealized conjunction of masculine and feminine principles. Anyone who recognizes that distinction can appreciate the mythic import of the parental couple without believing it is the authoritative and unchanging source of human reality. The problem is that being conscious of such a distinction is not normal. Being normal means mistaking heterosexuality for life itself.

Jiménez's position of authority is misleading to the degree that he pretends to have special access to a core truth. What he has instead of a solid grip on the only real reality is a very favorable position in a power relation with another human being. His symbolic authority is empty because he lacks the access to truth that he claims to possess, but socially and professionally, he functions just as well without it. He can do this because power does not act through human beings. It does not act at all, but materializes through the actions of human subjects in relation to one another (and in relation to nonhuman agents as well).

To succeed on terms a perversely skeptical reader like me would value, Jiménez would have to have what he wants his patient to have: the capacity to appreciate "differences between human beings and the diversity of realities that makes the world we speak of precisely a human world" (68). Jiménez falls short, but he reaches considerably farther in that direction than most people would dream of attempting. Whenever we fail to interest ourselves in other ways of being human, we inhabit a smaller and more fearful world, more like the post-apocalyptic nightmares that beset right-wing Christians.

3
Sexually Offensive Women

The more I have listened to women fumbling, usually in the dark, with their special problems, the more convinced I have become that as a caring society we need to bridge the large gap that exists between what we already know of female sexuality and the full truth about women and the vicissitudes of their sexual experience.

—Estela Welldon

Unleash your sexuality / on me

—k.d. lang, "Sexuality," *All You Can Eat*

Unauthorized pleasure

After college students staged Eve Ensler's (1998) *The Vagina Monologues* a couple of years ago as a benefit for a local sexual assault hotline, there was a contentious debate about a monologue based on a woman's memory of being seduced at the age of sixteen by a woman of twenty-four. "The Little Coochi Snorcher That Could" portrays the seduction as a blissful romp, and their encounter opens the door for the younger woman to heal from childhood sexual wounds. According to some audience members, "Coochi Snorcher" was offensive. It was inappropriate for a sexual assault hotline to allow its name to be associated with a performance that promoted the sexual abuse of a child. The young woman's delight did nothing to mitigate the offense. The monologue seemed to perpetuate the myths that women want to be raped and children are responsible when their elders sexually abuse them.

There was nothing in the lesbian seduction that hinted at aggression or coercion, but the critics believed that no matter how eager the younger woman was, the older woman committed a crime when she seduced her.[1] The lesbian's failure to adopt an asexual and maternal attitude was particularly damning. The younger woman, whose voice imbued the monologue with such joy, could only be a victim.

This is a perversion of the narrative. To make her into a victim, one must do exactly what Freud did: refuse to consider as authoritative a woman's account of herself. The young woman's monologue articulated plainly the differences between sexual abuse and sexual joy, but the story failed to follow the expected line. Happy and satisfied rather than devastated by what the lesbian did, the young woman did not fall in with what Jiménez called "*the psychic reality that we assume is shared by our fellows*" (67; italics in original).

The young women who produced the show, however, shared a different psychic reality. They were in the process of establishing a tradition that emphasizes women's freedom to enjoy their lives fully and take responsibility for their choices. Thanks to third-wave feminist icons like Eve Ensler, and because of their own experiences, these women were more ready than most of their elders to adopt liberal attitudes about sexual choice. They were familiar with current models of perpetrator and victim, so they had a secure foundation for articulating the difference between coercive and mutually satisfying sexual encounters. Because they were not inclined to discount the younger woman's account of her own sexual experience, it did not occur to them that the twenty-four-year-old seducer was exploitative or perverse.

The diverging interpretations of the young producers and the older audience members does not, of course, mean that the basic structures of the human mind have changed in one generation, such that the loyalty to the ideal "parental couple" that so recently defined our "shared reality" has been usurped in the younger generation by tolerance for perversion and exploitation. Much else has changed, however. Second-wave feminism emphasized the authority of the individual voice and clarified distinctions between consent, coercion, and violence, between active sexual pleasure and passive unresponsiveness, and between fixed, conventional categories of gender and our fluid human reality. Although second-wave feminism was often unkind to lesbians, the discourse it created made it harder to justify intolerance. Its origins mostly disowned or forgotten, the set of new meanings second-wave feminism created went on to inform queer conceptions of sexuality and gender, mainstream "women's magazine" attention to sexual violence and women's pleasure, and—the focus of this chapter—judicial and therapeutic approaches to sexual crime and perversion.

The past is still very much alive and in conflict with this evolution, and the outraged response of some older adults to "Coochi Snorcher" has much to do with the fact that the ideal "parental couple" has no place in the monologue. It is still the case that women's assertions of desire, especially lesbian desire, are difficult to assimilate to a shared reality in which an allegiance to reproductive heterosexuality is considered essential.

As a result, "lesbian" is still hard to reconcile with either "mother" or "child," so the meaning of "lesbian mother" is still indeterminate and suspect. Lesbian mothers have been targets of psychological studies and legal battles, discursive events that call up the specter of the potentially criminal, probably corrupting, female pervert. Richard Green (1992), psychiatrist, occasional expert witness, and prolific researcher on the psychology of sexuality and gender identity, concluded after a review of the literature that the children of lesbian mothers do not demonstrate more emotional problems, psychopathology, or gender confusion than the children of unpartnered heterosexual women. A relatively large community study (2003) affirmed that when psychologists unaware of the parents' sexual orientation evaluated children of lesbian, unpartnered heterosexual women, and heterosexual couples, they found no differences in the children's mental health or gendered behaviors.[2] That studies like this needed to be done at all speaks to the suspect status of lesbians as parents; that they have been conducted repeatedly since the 1970s suggests how difficult it has been to convince the courts that lesbian mothers represent no threat to their children's welfare.[3]

Transcripts of Green's testimony at the custody trial of a lesbian mother in Ohio in 1974 reveal an ironic edge to some of his answers. The mother's attorney asks Green, "how did the mother say she expresses herself regarding her sexual attraction to another female in front of the children?" Green replied: "She indicated that both she and [her partner] were particularly careful in terms of not exposing [the daughter] to explicit sex acts between the two of them" (25).[4] The testimony continued, covering at exhaustive length questions about whether the mother might induce the child to hate men, behave in a masculine fashion, or become a lesbian. On each point, Green reassured the court, testifying that the mother actually preferred men to women as companions and colleagues and encouraged her daughter to prefer men too (at age six, the girl had two boyfriends!). The mother gave her daughter Barbie dolls and wedding dresses to play with.

According to Green, the mother encouraged her daughter to adhere "to rather traditional stereotypic ways of what is considered to be 'appropriately' feminine" (25).

Green did not attempt to argue that lesbian sexuality is acceptable. Instead, he argued in essence that a lesbian mother can earn the right to raise her children by championing heterosexuality and striving to make her own orientation invisible. Not just her sexual acts but antisocial lesbian attitudes can be quarantined behind the doors of her bedroom; having turned that key, she can function in the rest of the house as a good enough mother.

What the court required, and Green supplied, was an evocation and denial of the many methods by which a perverse mother might thwart her daughter's normal heterosexual destiny. Asked whether there was a chance that the mother would molest her daughter sexually, Green replied, "Sexual molestation in our culture is pretty much by males . . . I would say the probability of child molestation is trivial" (29). His final hyperbolic prediction was that the daughter "will be a female feminine heterosexual lady" (27). The mother retained custody.

Green spoke with expert authority, but he was serving authorities higher on the judicial hierarchy than he. They determined the right questions to ask and what kinds of answers would be appropriate. Whatever Green might have been thinking about the tenor of the questioning, it was in the best interests of the mother and daughter that he addressed the situation of the lesbian mother from the safety of a shared human reality in which heterosexuality is the unquestioned foundation of social and familial order to which lesbians represent a limitable threat. Similarly, but armed with far less credibility than Green and with far more at stake, the lesbian mother had to prove that she was not a child molester.

Profiling the female sexual offender

Green's testimony emphasizes the rarity of the kind of sexual abuse the "Coochi Snorcher" seducer and the lesbian mothers were suspected of committing; that scarcity has made it difficult to identify and evaluate women who commit sexual crimes. For many decades, researchers have complained with ritual consistency about the dearth of research, especially empirical research, on female sexuality, perversion, and sexual offenses, typically attributing that lack either to low incidence or to society's reluctance to imagine women as capable of perversions or sexual crimes.[5]

Some researchers have denied their own limited data in order to implicate women as sexual abusers of children; they suggest that most boys who are sexually abused by women don't report it to anyone, or that mothers hide their sexual abuse of children so well that no one, not even the victims, can identify it.[6] Most researchers agree, however, that the few female offenders they can identify don't fit the models developed to explain the motivations and behavior patterns of male offenders. For one thing, most women who sexually abuse children commit their crimes in the presence of a male co-offender.

Reinforcing the difficulty finding a group large enough to generalize about, social workers Christiansen and Thyer (2002) cite estimates of the number of female perpetrators that range from 6 percent to 18 percent of the total, but they admit that there is no way to be certain. Nevertheless, they set up categories of female offenders that describe their backgrounds and motives. The "Teacher/Lover Offender" is most like the older woman in "Coochi Snorcher," but women in this category target adolescent male victims. Matthews, Mathews, and Speltz (1991), working in psychology and the criminal justice system, also presented an ambitious "typology" based on a small sample of female sexual offenders. They reported that Teacher/Lover Offenders think of their relation to the victim in idealized and romantic terms, failing to understand that they are abusers. The question of whether the boys felt victimized remains unanswered.

Of the twelve female sexual offenders Nathan and Ward (respectively, a clinical psychologist and a criminologist) examined, nine committed their crimes in the presence of male offenders who were fathers, stepfathers, or involved in sexual relationships with the women (2002). Some of the female offenders had sex with men in front of the victim, or, while the male offender watched, had oral or penetrative sex with the victim. Because three of the twelve women had "previous adult *sexual* relationships with other adult females," the authors theorize that "deviant arousal" is a significant motivator among female offenders (15; italics in original).

Seeking to understand the mind of the perpetrator, Nathan and Ward tested the women for psychological disorders and found among the pathologies "some rebellion against the female role and some ambivalence about heterosexual relations" (17–18). Eight of the women had been sexually abused as children by men, but Nathan and Ward did not propose that those women might have reason to be ambivalent about heterosexuality, or that prior experiences of abuse might affect their ability to know the difference between sexual abuse and healthy sexuality.

Nathan and Ward do not describe what "the female role" comprises, but the conventional understanding requires women to exhibit the desire to nurture children and some degree of submission to male authority. Most of the female offenders Nathan and Ward examined were faced with a choice between these fundamental aspects of the conventional female role. They made the worst possible choice, not only failing to protect the children in their care, but actively participating in their victimization.

As things are now, women who fail to protect children from predatory men are considered as guilty as women who abuse children themselves. This is so even though some of the predators they are supposed to defend against turn out to be husbands, boyfriends, and male relatives, the very same people who, according to other patriarchal regulations, women are duty bound to trust with the job of defending them and their children from the depredations of other men. Any woman who adheres closely to traditional femininity will be gravely handicapped if she ever faces a conflict between protecting her children and submitting to male authority. Statistically, women are more likely to experience male violence within the family than anywhere else in their lives, so that conflict is not as rare as it should be.

Mother at the root

Psychoanalyst Estela Welldon (1988), whose ideas have been cited in the literature on female perverts and perpetrators, attempted to fill some of the gaps in the story of the female pervert by developing a psychoanalytic theory of female perversion.[7] She followed a conventional psychoanalytic line by defining perversion as a form of hatred and arguing that lesbians are failed heterosexuals who, in their love relationships with women, attempt to regress to "an early relationship with their mothers" (99, 44). According to Welldon, perversions and homosexuality arise when that early relationship goes wrong, but she did not identify "homosexuality" specifically as a perversion. Instead she pointed to the suggestion of another psychoanalyst that mothers who commit incest with children of either sex are homosexual (99).

Welldon's vision of female perversion is so expansive that she sees eating disorders, repeated cosmetic surgery, shoplifting, prostitution, and self-mutilation as female perversions; that, at least, inflates the number of potential subjects sufficiently to give interested parties something to theorize about.

Citing Luce Irigaray's assertion that "woman has sex organs just about everywhere," Welldon claimed that "in women perversion operates fully through their bodies as whole [*sic*]" (34). Once perversion gains a foothold, it behaves like old-fashioned hysteria, migrating throughout the female body and producing the particular signs that best express the woman's distress. The perverse signs need not involve sexual arousal or sexual content, except to the extent that a psychoanalyst assigns sexual meaning to diverse phenomena.

In contrast with some of the psychologists and criminologists who cite her, Welldon did not attempt to organize this profusion of signs into a rational system of classification. Instead she identified the mother as the singular source of miscellaneous pathologies, thus joining a long psychoanalytic tradition. Beginning with Richard von Krafft-Ebing's natural history of perversion, *Psychopathia Sexualis* (1886), sexological studies suggested that the origins of feminine "perversion" could be found in a woman's early relationship with her mother. Long before Richard Green defended mothers against charges of sexual and social corruption, Krafft-Ebing cited the case of a homosexual woman who, as a child, slept beside her mother, whom Krafft-Ebing identifies as a "Messalina" (416). (He was probably alluding to Messalina's legendary promiscuity rather than her penchant for political intrigue, but both facets speak to fears about the destructive power of the seductive mother.) Later, in his study of a young lesbian, Freud followed a similar line, remarking, "the analysis revealed beyond all shadow of doubt that the beloved lady was a substitute for—the mother."

Even those who believe a homosexual life can be viable agree that early mother-daughter relationships are at the root of women's sexual desire for women. This assumption gives therapy a direction, in that any problems lesbians experience in intimate relationships can be ascribed to an unhealthy revival of pre-oedipal symbiosis with the mother, which can be worked through in analysis.[8] Beverly Burch (1993), a feminist psychoanalyst who has worked extensively with lesbians, claimed that most important achievement, the thing that readies a girl for healthy sexuality (and by implication prevents perversion), is to separate sufficiently from the mother to regard her as "Other in a nontraumatic way" (92). She manages this by identifying to at least some degree with the father, because fathers represent autonomy, separate selfhood, and the ability to take action.[9] She needs this cross-sex identification because the infant's pre-oedipal experience of the mother is inchoate and dependent, hardly a sturdy framework for any adult sexuality. Whether antilesbian, feminist, or "woman-centered," theories that favor pre-oedipal explanations feature lesbians who suffer from a lack of personal boundaries in intimate relationships and who repeatedly succumb to hatred and self-disgust, affects left over from early traumas. How would so fragile a psyche avoid perversion?

Although Burch approved the multifaceted nature of sexuality, her ideas about healthy and unhealthy choices of sexual object were subject to narrow guidelines. The main locus of concern remained the unseparated mother, although Burch also listed feminist interests and gender skepticism as possible contributors to lesbian development, thus offering a neutral version of the suspicions others have expressed about lesbians and other female perverts being man-haters and resisting "the female role."

Identifying the mother and daughter as the central relationship of the perverse system has had strange effects on studies of mothers' involvement in paternal sexual abuse. It is common to accuse a mother of complicity in the sexual abuse of daughters by their fathers or other men, even if they did not know of the abuse. Unlike the women Nathan and Ward examined, these mothers are not perpetrators. Their guilt is inferred from the father's crime. Psychologists Rucker and Lombardi (1990) brought the assumption of maternal complicity to an absurd extreme when they claimed that "father-daughter molestation may be seen as an enactment of erotic urges and fantasies between mother and daughter that find origin in pre-Oedipal, mother-child qualities of relatedness" (99). It hardly needs saying that Rucker and Lombardi think that unconscious female homosexual fantasies are the root of the trouble, but it is harder to imagine what satisfactions the mother and daughter found in "seducing" the father into unwittingly acting out their desires for each other.

Claudia Card (1995) noted early in her chapter on "female incest" that she has not "found lesbian-*identified* women who were *sexual* abusers of children." Like Welldon, Card argued that almost any maternal practice could be incestuous, including any behavior involved in "care-taking, punishment, or affection" (134). Amid the burgeoning possibilities, Card tried to establish the "contexts of female incest" by citing an instance of the torture and murder of a child by a female babysitter and alluding uncritically to reports of sexual abuse and murder of children in satanic cults.[10] Venturing even further afield, Card speculated that anything from "conflicts within feminist organizations, conferences, and classrooms" to "lesbian stalking . . . might have roots in childhood female incest" (145).

To these ephemera Card added instances of documented maternal sexual abuse in which mothers engaged in "clitoral stimulation of daughters, sometimes encouraging daughters to reciprocate" (135). In spite of the clear (and clearly criminal) incestuous behaviors in these cases, she continued to think it was even more difficult to imagine what behaviors would constitute "female incest" than it was to imagine "what lesbians do" when they have sex (135).

Why is it so hard to say, at least in the discourse on female perversion, what maternal incest is or what lesbians do? First, psychoanalytic theory, along with much of the "woman-centered" or even feminist theory that derives from it, cannot effectively distinguish lesbian sex from incest or sexual from nonsexual behaviors. This inability or refusal to differentiate also means that "perversions," evident emotional problems, and any real crimes women commit can be attributed to nebulous maternal motives. We do not accuse men who commit incest of peculiarly paternal crimes; most generously they are thought to be motivated by misdirected, but otherwise normal, sexual desire; more stringent observers note perpetrators' claims of male entitlement to female sexual service and the easy negation of the victim's full humanity. Whatever motivations are ascribed to the male perpetrators, few have trouble describing specific criminal sexual acts.

The perverse, incestuous mother, by contrast, is an odd phantom whose crimes are at once legion and unimaginable; nevertheless, she haunts the psychology of female sexuality. When anything a woman does can be taken as evidence of perversion, when any significant problem a daughter experiences can be attributed to maternal perversion, when lesbians are by definition locked in a cycle of incestuous love and hate with "the mother," and when evidence that a child has been abused sexually by anyone can be used to implicate the mother as a guilty party, then it no longer makes sense to differentiate the perpetrators from the victims. As mothers, as daughters, as women, we stand accused of—something.

The perverse child

Robert Stoller, a leading psychoanalytic theorist of perversion, recommended that interested researchers "observe the parents, especially mothers, of the people whose behavior is the object of our research . . . for the insight it gives into the pressures brought to bear on the child who is to become aberrant . . . One will understand the origins of perversion best if one views it as blighted heterosexuality" (xvii).

Stoller realized that psychoanalysts had not defined what normal heterosexuality was, but he worked under the assumption that, whatever it was, it was a part of the child from the beginning and was his destiny. Stoller could call upon normal heterosexuality to justify his authoritative statements about perversion not in spite, but because heterosexuality did not require definition, so high was it on the hierarchy of sexual value that one hardly even had to speak its name. And yet, heterosexuality turns fragile when faced with the threat of sexual perversion.

Stoller would later rethink his initial position and produce some of the most exciting and conscientious work on sexual diversity and its vicissitudes that anyone has attempted, but his early definition of perversion is still standard among psychoanalysts. Perversion is "a habitual, preferred aberration necessary for one's full satisfaction, primarily motivated by hostility" which is "a state in which one wishes to harm an object . . . The hostility in perversion takes form in a fantasy of revenge hidden in the actions that make up the perversion and serves to convert childhood trauma to adult triumph" (5).

In Stoller's early work, perversion expressed itself in a relatively orderly fashion imitative of, and responsive to, heterosexual patterns. The organized relation of perversion to heterosexuality gave it coherence and allowed it to be identified as a clinical entity.[11] In Stoller's view, perversion acted conservatively, preserving the status quo by making the perverse child bear the burden of the parents' hostility, so that the parents can continue to function as if they were normal. In the absence of such a child, the perverse family system would implode under the weight of its own unvented hostility. If the family provides the essential pattern of social coherence, and the perverse child is the bulwark that prevents its collapse into disorder, then society cannot survive without its perverse progeny. By the same token, the shared fantasy of the parental couple's goodness and vitality could not long survive the recognition that what passes for normal heterosexuality generates perversion. Denial is vital.

The only way to preserve normal heterosexuality was to police its boundaries, defining as perversion anything that might be excluded from the unexamined center. Heterosexuality, therefore, was not a form of erotic hatred; it was not compulsive, and it was not homosexual.

Ten years after *Perversion*, Stoller (1985) wrote that heterosexuality was no less complicated than homosexuality, so it could not be used "as the standard of health, normality, mature genital characterhood, or whatever other ambiguous criterion serves one's philosophy these days" (101–2). What had seemed to be the norm was instead people living out complex lives in relation to an idealized heterosexuality. The boundaries between normality and the perverse, which had seemed clear enough when heterosexuality went unexamined, were now harder to determine. Across the sexualities, there was potential for benign and harmful variation, fantasies of restitution or revenge, the replaying of traumas and the discovery of joy and intimacy.

Stoller's awareness of the hostile social dynamic that affects the perverse child was already apparent in *Perversion*, when he asserted that moralistic approaches to perversion were wrong. About employing homosexuality as a diagnosis, Stoller commented, "there would be no diagnosis of homosexuality—only the myriad forms of homosexual behavior would be recognized—if the bigotry of the righteous did not force the belief (shared even by homosexuals) that a distinct essence—homosexuality—exists" (201).[12] Stoller's assertion that there was no essential homosexuality led to the recognition that there was no essential heterosexuality either, but it also prevented him from recognizing that asserting a minority sexual identity can have positive personal and social effects. In 1975, when Stoller made these comments, the gay liberation movement was well underway; one of its chief accomplishments was to promote identity labels that had neither diagnostic nor legal implications, but functioned (albeit incompletely and problematically) as rallying points for social and political communities.

Declaring homosexual identities invalid at the time Stoller did so left human identity tethered to the mother ship of heterosexuality. Like the preoedipal mother, heterosexuality signified a totality from which one could not separate because there is no self outside the totality. As the infant's core self was the mother, the homosexual's core self was heterosexual. Neither the infant nor the homosexual had the capacity to recognize the nature of their dependence, because neither had yet recognized the irreducible meaning of sexual difference. The difference is that babies grow up. Homosexuals never do unless they become heterosexual.

There was no room in the standard psychoanalytic line for terms of positive identification like "lesbian" or "gay." As a behavior if not an identity, bisexuality was less problematic because it implied at least a half measure of openness to heterosexuality. The later permutation, "queer," would seem to align well with psychoanalysis because it recognizes the fluidity of identity and behavior, but "queer" saw all sexual identities as equally totalizing and all subjects as equally in need of deconstruction.

Stoller defined an activity as perverse "if the erotic excitement depends on one's feeling that one is sinning" (1985, 7). But if perversion acts throughout familial and social systems, then one's erotic excitement could just as well depend on the feeling that someone else is sinning. When the range of permitted pleasures is so narrow that the slightest deviation in thought or behavior calls forth the fear that one is sinning against God or nature's heterosexual ideal, it must be comforting to be able to give the specter a name other than one's own. If necessary, one can either deny the validity of lesbian and gay identities or appoint a homosexual subject to denigrate or pity. Either way, homosexuality functions as the "habitual, preferred aberration necessary for [heterosexuality's] full satisfaction," but it is impolitic to acknowledge that, because both homosexuality and heterosexuality arise in an environment that is hostile to homosexual behaviors and identities (1985, 9). A theory of sexual development that fails to consider the social impact of ubiquitous antagonism to homosexuality cannot fully understand the perverse aspects of normal heterosexuality; nor can it begin to grasp how politically and personally useful it can be, therefore, to refuse to be deconstructed and insist instead that one's minority identity is authentic and essential.

Women who grow up to be children

Stoller believed that female homosexuality was less hostile than the male variety, and questioned whether that was due to the female homosexual's "knowing she is a female like her mother" (1975, 202). Asserting that she is female seems like a fairly basic place to begin, although radical feminist and queer theory would at once limit her femaleness and extend it to anyone who might wish to claim it. Identifying her with her mother tethers her firmly to heterosexuality, whatever that is. There is nothing, not even a remarkable level of hostility, to identify her even as a clinical entity, a female homosexual. Still less is she a sexual, political, and social entity such as a lesbian.

In antilesbian schools of psychoanalysis, however, the relation between the two other terms—mother and female homosexual—is visible only as a manifestation of deep, even murderous aggression. Charles Socarides

(1970) cited other psychoanalysts who agreed with him on the essential hostility of female homosexuality (128). The mothers, however, were not innocent victims but perpetrators. They prohibited masturbation, or were aggressive, controlling, neglectful, sadistic, or smothering; they rejected their daughters for being female. For these reasons, their daughters became female homosexuals.

As a prelude to his discussion, in the year after the Stonewall riot, a landmark event for the gay pride movement that made claims to authentic identity a key political strategy, Socarides (1970) attempted to establish psychiatry's exclusive rights to define homosexuality: "It is vitally important to realize this fundamental point: the diagnosis of homosexuality can not be self-made, imposed by jurists, articulated by clergy, or speculated about by social scientists" (1202).

Having cleared the field of all those unqualified to comment, Socarides furnished an authoritative account. The female lover was a "mother-substitute," as Freud said, and hatred was the emotion that defined both the infantile and the "adult" relationship (132). Any female homosexual who claimed to love her mother (or mother-substitute) actually hated her. Any female homosexual who hated her mother also wanted to return to infancy and merge with her. Any female homosexual who professed to feel indifference or tolerance or affection toward her mother in fact both hated and desired to merge with her. For Socarides and his ilk, female homosexuality existed only within the confines of the drive to merge with and destroy the mother. The status of the female homosexual, therefore, was that of an emotional and sexual infant, monstrous for being housed in the body of an adult female.[13] Prospects were especially bleak for "obligatory homosexuals," or women who refused to have sex with men. Socarides felt that female homosexuals who did have sex with men were more likely to become heterosexual. Among the minority of psychiatrists and psychologists who still believe that homosexuality is a profound disorder and/or that it can be cured, Socarides is an important, indeed revered, source of wisdom.[14]

Refusing to acknowledge an effective lesbian identity, and continuing to promote the model of a "female homosexual" who is actually an angry and undeveloped female heterosexual, accomplishes quite a bit. From a conservative perspective, female heterosexuality represents the highest degree of social and sexual maturity a woman can attain, but defining such an ideal precisely is difficult in the first place, and the result is vulnerable to deconstructive collapse. The provision of a suitably pathological foil, as

Stoller recognized in his discussion of perverse family dynamics, allows the ideal to escape that fate. All that negative energy can be redirected to the perverse "child," who would become useless as a container for hostility if she succeeded in asserting a sexual, political, and social identity of her own. The female homosexual therefore has much in common with the female sexual offender, in that habeas corpus does not apply; no one need actually produce one in order to pass judgment.

The most dire threat, however, awaits those who neither move toward normal heterosexuality nor remain in the pervert's corner. For them, psychosis awaits. In the latter twentieth century, while biological explanations turned to genetic and/or hormonal deviations from the heterosexual norm, there appeared a number of discussions placing psychosis in some relation to homosexuality, with infantilism mediating the connection. Psychosis represents a dissolution of the personality or selfhood of an individual. A psychotic individual loses her ability to think or function. Antilesbian psychology sometimes asserts that homosexuality is an etiological factor in psychosis, but homosexuality also seems to function as a defense, so that the beleaguered psyche of the female homosexual faces a choice between perversion and profound disintegration.

Feminist discourses have not given much attention to defending the lesbian from accusations of infantilism and psychosis, but Judith Butler made the attempt in response to Julia Kristeva, for whom, as Butler put it, "the unmediated cathexis of female homosexual desire leads unequivocally to psychosis" (86). A mediated homosexual desire would manifest (or rather, ultimately fail to manifest as such) mainly through motherhood, which takes a woman to the edge of homosexual psychosis but allows her to save her sanity by giving birth to a baby, which is a substitute for a penis, which in its turn represents the father, who—as Beverly Burch averred—can save the lesbian daughter by giving her something to identify with. Butler wrote that patriarchal law "is precisely the mechanism that produces the construct of lesbianism as a site of irrationality. Significantly, this description of lesbian experience is effected from the outside and tells us more about the fantasies that a fearful heterosexual culture produces to defend against its own homosexual possibilities than about lesbian experience itself" (87).

The theory of lesbian psychosis helps preserve patriarchy for the same reasons that heterosexuality requires its perverse counterpart: to prevent the onset of its own full-fledged psychosis. But why should Butler, who has so masterfully deconstructed categories of gender and sexuality, refer uncritically to "lesbian experience itself" and imagine that lesbianism has an inside and an outside? My own first response to the lesbian psychosis theory was to consider all the lesbians I know and build a case based on their proven ability to form healthy relationships and hold down jobs. Then I reviewed studies that, going a step further than Richard Green, give credence to the hypothesis that lesbians are as emotionally healthy as heterosexual women. In sum, I tried to consolidate a lesbian identity and community, gathering evidence that lesbians function about as well as heterosexuals. All this to defend against the doubtful proposal that one can only dodge psychosis by having or being the phallus—in other words, by accepting as true and universally applicable one particular cultural myth about the supreme power of masculinity.

From the psychoanalytic point of view, the doubts I've just expressed about that proposal are symptomatic of an intellectual and/or psychological deficit, a failure to function. An exchange between Socarides and Nanette Gartrell, then an instructor in psychiatry at Harvard Medical School, demonstrates the tragic ultimate consequences of not getting it. Gartrell observed that studies of nonpatient populations of lesbians showed them to be at least as well-adjusted as single heterosexual women. In response, Socarides tendered this indictment: "Pathology, organically and psychologically, may be defined as a failure to function . . . . It is this failure, its significance, and manifold consequences that are so obvious in obligatory homosexuality—a failure of functioning which, if carried to its extreme, would mean the death of the species" (510).

Like the figure of Justice holding the scales, the psychoanalyst balances this calamitous vision against his earlier contention that no one but psychiatrists are qualified to comment on the meaning of homosexuality. He is the antithesis of the pathological failure to function; in fact, with his reasoned opinion in hand, he stands to save not only the individual woman or even the institution of heterosexuality, but the entire species.

Gartrell's response to Socarides was included in the same issue. She did not challenge, or even acknowledge, his apocalyptic scenario. Instead, she cited studies in which lesbians scored higher than heterosexual women in terms of job stability and satisfaction, self-actualization, and self-confidence. She responded as I first wanted to respond to the lesbian psychosis theory, by demonstrating that lesbians function well. In the decades since their exchange was published, it has become clearer that although lesbians' rate of unplanned pregnancy is rather low, they function well in the reproductive arena and could, if the need arose, prevent species extinction.

Gartrell herself has made major contributions to the literature on lesbian families.

For his part, Socarides' apocalyptic fantasy is typical of the right-wing sexual and reproductive politics Stoller (and probably Gartrell) would repudiate, but the idea that homosexuality is a threat to the vitality of the heterosexual couple is shared more generally, as evidenced by the support for the 1996 Defense of Marriage Act, the passage of a slew of state laws in 2004 to outlaw same-sex marriage, and the renewal during selected election seasons of calls for state and federal constitutional amendments banning same-sex marriage. Efforts like Gartrell's to normalize homosexuality have influenced psychologists and psychiatrists, and general heterosexual tolerance for sexual "others" is on the rise, but voting patterns continue to show that many heterosexuals continue to be uneasy about the integrity of their institution.[15]

All of those who have a stake in these scenarios of sexuality, family, and apocalypse—including Gartrell, Socarides, me, liberals, the religious right, the judicial system, heterosexuals, and queers—are attempting to garner some degree of social power. The only way one can be sure of possessing power is to exercise it. Discovering some object to exercise power on is more than tempting; it's essential. It matters to some degree whether the object of the exercise recognizes one's authority and believes it to be benign, but if she doesn't, one can ascribe her lack of cooperation to pathologies or moral failings. In contrast to Gartrell, for Socarides the idea that a lesbian could be happy and do well is literally unthinkable. It is unthinkable for him because the existence of a lesbian like that unseats him from what he believes to be his rightful, even heroic, place in social, professional, and familial hierarchies. The prospect of women not including the heterosexual male in scenes of sexual desire, reproduction, and family is so frightful that Socarides equates it with the extinction of the species.

The figure of the heterosexual mother is important for Socarides because she stands between him and the unthinkable beyond. She is what the female homosexual must become. However, the heterosexual mother is an undependable figure, as likely to be the portal to destruction as a guardian against it. When she fails to teach her daughters to be heterosexual, when she fails to preserve heterosexual male power, the psychiatric professional must intercede and repair the damage. The goal of treatment, at least, is simple: the female homosexual daughter must be converted into the heterosexual mother, so that she can experience "the affective state of love, tenderness, and joy with a partner of the opposite sex" (Socarides, 511).

Leslie Deutsch (1995) might have been diagnosing the clinical scene in which Socarides delivers the cure when she questioned whether it is "any accident that women with severe pathology . . . should enter treatment with analysts who are likely to see the patients' sexuality as inherently pathological? For a lesbian to enter treatment with a homophobic clinician is as problematic as for a black patient to be treated by a racist therapist, and it should raise questions about the patient's judgment, internalized self-hatred, and masochism" (31).

The woman who enrolls as a female homosexual patient with an antihomosexual therapist agrees to serve his needs. What he needs, all unconsciously and in accordance with the laws of countertransference (the clinical version of the perverse family dynamic Stoller described) is for her to be deeply troubled and in need of rescue. The figure of the female homosexual is as much a pawn as that of the perverse child. What she lacks is specifically the means to refuse to serve in the role assigned to her.

In an essay on the situation of the "dyke" in feminist theory, Caroline Dever shows how a lesbian consciousness might understand the word metaphorically:

> The function of the dyke is to enable another activity, such as the holding or conducting of water, but [it] is essentially passive: it exists primarily not as a presence but as an absence, as negative space sculpted from the positive surface of the earth. Yet in its alternate definition, the dyke exceeds that positive surface, existing as the highly visible surplus of earth in fortifying relation to the populace whose existence it protects and enables . . . the well-being of its architects depends on the dyke's structural integrity. (20)

Dever was speaking to the particular dynamics of liberal feminism, but her metaphor fits as well with Stoller's vision of the function of the pervert, who serves "four necessities: preservation of the individual's pleasure, preservation of the family, preservation of society, and preservation of the species" (1975, 215). There she is, the pervert at the mouth of hell, where it is her treacherous job to hold back chaos and to be chaos, to both preserve and undermine the species and its institutions. It seems a lot to ask, particularly as the in-service dyke and/or female homosexual has little left over for the individual pleasures Stoller mentions.

There is hope, however. According to Stoller, a "perversion . . . that starts out as a defender of the status quo will gradually be elaborated, with scarcely a wrench, into a radical agent of change" (1975, 217). Stoller did not say what radical changes that revolution would produce, nor did he describe how those changes could come about "with scarcely a wrench," but whenever the revolution does come around, it will probably not mean the end of the world. Nominally monogamous, reproductive heterosexuality already survives well in the absence of universal compliance, so the chances are small that it will become extinct when the dyke retires or refuses to serve. How, then, will the anti-homosexual movement sustain itself? Those with the biggest investment in anti-homosexual discourse, including those who are sincerely panicked and those who cynically exploit prejudice for political gain, are part of a perverse construction in Stoller's sense of a collective expression of erotic hatred, exercised compulsively on a designated object. The social perversion maintains things as they are, but it brings no more than a sickly pleasure to a few and misery (paranoia, self-hatred, violence, broken families, divided churches) to many.

Resolving the perversion means moving into a post-apocalyptic realm where one can acknowledge outright that heterosexuality is self-perpetuating, that it needs neither rhetorical defense nor legal protection. The next step toward revolution is recognizing that there is a world of difference between normal sexual diversity and the ways that people use sexuality to destructive ends. Perverse behaviors are ubiquitous in the sense that even people in unexceptional heterosexual relationships must have the courage to venture out of the narrow confines of idealized heterosexuality in order to become sexually mature and experience pleasure, trust, and intimacy. It is not nearly as difficult as Welldon or Card imply to differentiate consensual sexual exploration from the violence done to body and spirit in criminal sexual abuse; nor does it tax the mind very much to make a distinction between sexual acts and maternal care or organizational infighting. Fumbling such distinctions means that anything we do, and any pleasant or unpleasant experience we have, might turn out to have been a crime. Fearing to do unwitting harm and fearing to be a victim keep the potential revolutionary from taking a step in her own direction. Liberal feminism, the almost normal sister the dyke is assigned to protect, has been particularly ready to succumb to immobilizing self-accusation.

Surmounting these considerable obstacles would move us closer to resolving our socially perverse dynamic and arriving in a more rational world. The local producers of *The Vagina Monologues* exemplify what it means to take steps in that direction. It is hard to imagine what the world would be like after the revolution, when everyone had abandoned the fantasy that her or his sexual identity was evidence of personal merit, psychological normality, or spiritual superiority; when it would no longer make sense to think of one's sexual desires as a map of universal mind or a guide to the ideal family structure, when the sex of one's lover would make one neither the central ornament of human reality nor a living specter in a perverse nightmare. A world without all that would at least be a less violent world.

4
Making Theoretical Space

I must get to those spaces:
black space of throathole
brown space of asshole
red space of cunthole
sex space of no turning back

Stomach
take me to them
and lead me in a good song
—Cheryl Clarke, "Space Invocation"

A negative space was soon formed about my person.
—Sigmund Freud

The best defense

A deluge of articles using psychoanalysis appeared in the last decade in the humanities and psychology, evidence that psychoanalysis has gripped the imaginations and suited the research projects of scholars in many fields.[1] Yet I also know other scholars who, having been introduced to psychoanalysis at some point in their careers, consider it a dead end. These others are less likely to write journal articles addressing their intimidation by, lack of interest in, ignorance of, or distaste for psychoanalysis.

Psychoanalysis thus appears to be an either/or proposition: one either gets it and uses it, or one doesn't. Scholars who use psychoanalysis—the insiders—disagree about what "getting it" means, and they criticize psychoanalytic theory, revise it, and even (as in the cases of Luce Irigaray or Judith Butler) subvert it. "Not getting it," however, means a choice to turn one's back on the network of psychoanalytic theories. Viewed from an outsider's perspective, psychoanalysis surrounds itself with a defensive screen of arcane language and homage to a founding father. The screen is permeable, but only in one direction.

"I don't get it," a colleague said when we talked about this chapter. "Why would you want to waste your time promoting something so oppressive?" It's a fair question. Wherever psychoanalysis addresses developmental issues or describes the structure of the psyche, it can claim to illuminate the essential inner mysteries even of its outsiders. In 1978, Nancy Chodorow wrote that psychoanalysis, in spite of its problems, was the most credible theory available for grasping "fundamental aspects of the psychology of women" (142).

Psychoanalysis still offers some of the richest and best-sustained analyses available. It would be difficult to understand current patterns of thinking about women's sexuality in Europe and the United States without engaging with psychoanalysis. Psychoanalysis is imbricated in those patterns and participates in the silences, policing of thought, and distortions that afflict debates generally about the issue of "feminine personality" and women's sexuality. Because psychoanalysis is the most powerful analytic engine currently in use for understanding women's sexuality, both academic and clinical participants in psychoanalytic discourses must engage in continual reassessment and critique of the most basic assumptions about how women desire. Even more important, they must consider how the machinery of theory production determines its effects.

What I want to do is slit the divide between psychoanalytic insiders and outsiders, making it permeable in both directions so that I can address the part of psychoanalytic theory that has most troubled me: sexual difference and its implications for lesbian development and sexuality.[2] Although being a lesbian is no bar to "getting" psychoanalysis, psychoanalysis in both its clinical and academic modes has a history of quarantining homosexuality and homosexuals. Noreen O'Connor and Joanna Ryan (1993) wrote, "Psychoanalysis, as a body of theory and practice, has not been able to integrate homosexuality into itself. Instead, homosexuality remains largely split off, inadequately discussed and understood, subject to rigid and sometimes attacking theorising, and to excluding practices" (9). I would say instead that psychoanalysis *has* integrated homosexuality, but as a site for the performance of exclusions that are crucial for maintaining the "body of theory and practice" that is psychoanalysis. O'Connor and Ryan later suggested that the silences in psychoanalytic theory mark divisions between the theorists and the other, the female homosexual-as-excluded-other, whose discourse is contained within the silences. Admitting her voice would "require psychoanalytic theory to change" (1993, 265).

I would state the case less moderately: The body of psychoanalysis would be transformed into something hardly recognizable if it ceased placing homosexuality under quarantine. Under the influence of these exclusions—those that have affected me directly and those that result from the identities psychoanalysis ascribes to me—I find that I am less concerned about whether any given claim about sexual difference and lesbian development is "correct" and more interested in the politics of theoretical authority. Specifically, what does it mean for a theoretical claim to occupy an authoritative position? Where do excluded claims go? Can a discourse that produces unauthorized claims actualize them in some separate "insider's" space of its own? In pursuit of answers, I begin by mapping the conceptual and rhetorical space that determines who is authorized to participate as a maker of theory in psychoanalytic discourses and by what means they establish that authority. My own unauthorized account of sexual difference erupts at the midpoint, and I use it to position a persona of its maker on the discursive map. Finally, by looking for tools to slit the divide and create a more comfortable space for that persona, I locate some alternative ways of conceiving lesbian sexual difference in contemporary fiction and poetry.

The phrase "lesbian sexual difference" may create difficulty for those who think of sexual difference as referring ultimately to stable anatomical differences between men and women. Those differences have unpredictable effects, but they are the bedrock of meaning. The objection is that "lesbian sexual difference" is impossible because it does not stand on the foundation of male/female difference. Lesbians among themselves can't represent sexual difference. Psychoanalysis has sometimes identified that apparent lack of difference as the problem with lesbians: if desire can only occur where there is sexual difference, and there is no sexual difference between women, then there can be no desire between women. "Lesbian sexual difference" has been inadmissible to reason because (unlike "lesbian sexuality") it asserts a difference of its own, claiming to authorize what sexual difference prohibits.

The idea that sexual difference is at its root heterosexual often goes unquestioned, but it is possible to recognize the dominance of heterosexual forms without ascribing to them the power to determine the meaning of everyone's desire. First, if anatomical differences between men and women are the bedrock of heterosexual desire, then *sexual difference* should be rendered as *heterosexual difference.* Second, because it is a term with a more limited application, *heterosexual difference* concedes some theoretical space that *lesbian sexual difference* might occupy. Lesbian sexual difference indicates the possibility of relations of desire between women based on embodied sexual difference that cannot be comprehended from within the most common definitions of heterosexual difference. Women's bodies and genitalia differ greatly in color, shape, size, scent, and texture. These differences lack symbolic significance in heterosexual theory, in part because difference conceived as duality makes it difficult to appreciate the interplay of multiple differences.

Debates about the validity of conventional patterns of domination/subordination and symbolic sufficiency/insufficiency have dominated interpretations of heterosexual difference and lesbian sexuality, but it is not possible to understand the effects on lesbian desire of the differences among women's sexual bodies by invoking these patterns. Lesbians engage in domination and subordination in their sexual and social lives, and they often use heterosexual frameworks for interpreting their sexual bodies and practices. However, lesbian desire is not locked into the penis/vagina duality that is so essential to shoring up heterosexual difference and desire.

At this point lesbian sexual difference can neither be cut loose nor assimilated within heterosexual frameworks. It seems unnecessary to work hard at establishing an anatomical basis for lesbian desire that would rival the power of anatomical heterosexual difference to define heterosexual desire. The ambiguity of lesbian sexual difference suits my purpose, which is to investigate how theorists establish or refute theoretical authority in psychoanalysis and monitor insider/outsider status.

Inside authority

Freud's published lecture "Femininity" (1933) exemplified the permeable barrier between the psychoanalyst and his audience, whose innermost psychic structures were theoretically open to him.[3] Freud began by identifying the audience as outsiders. Although he proposed to offer only "observed facts, almost without any speculative additions," he anticipated that even this would be excessive: "for you I am saying too much and saying things which you are not equipped to understand and which are not in your province" (112). Women were in effect excluded, for unlike men, they were not supposed to worry about the problem that "Femininity" addressed. Freud suggested that women over thirty, exhausted by the "difficult development to femininity," suffer from a "psychical rigidity" that makes them unable to benefit fully from psychoanalysis (134–35). Even "our excellent women colleagues" were sidelined by heterosexual difference, as male analysts allowed female analysts token insider status by absolving them of feminine flaws and extending to them partial and honorary membership in the masculine set (116–17).[4] At the end of the lecture, having affirmed that for the most part, women's "nature is determined by their sexual function," Freud remarked that "we do not overlook the fact that an individual woman may be a human being in other respects as well" (135). He did not, however, suggest what aspects of a woman's life other than her "sexual function" might define her humanity.

Given the successive exclusions and caveats in regard to the agency of heterosexual women, it is difficult to imagine from this on what basis female homosexuals might entreat for inclusion in the theoretical discourse. Although Freud asserted that the "greater amount of activity" of female homosexuals is a masculine characteristic, the activity of female homosexuals is a pretense. They "play the parts of mother and baby as often and as clearly as those of husband and wife" (130). As these are the relations that define a woman's "sexual function" and therefore her humanity, it is significant that female homosexuals can only pretend to participate in them.

Of all theorists, Judith Butler has done the most to undermine the assumption that a stable, material, binary sexual difference underlies the performance of gender roles. A postmodern "Butlerian" consciousness would recognize that the roles of husband and wife as well as mother and child lack authenticity no matter who is playing them. However, the consequence of playing these roles in an unauthorized context is that one appears to have no basis from which to speak or act. The resistance I've encountered from psychoanalysts and feminists in the humanities to the idea of a *lesbian sexual difference* suggests that heterosexual difference is still felt to be the natural or at least inevitable basis of meaning. Thus *lesbian sexual difference* seems not only incoherent, but disrespectful—a way of using language to behave badly by attempting to render psychoanalysis meaningless.

As Butler (1990) described the topography of the coherent subject, "'Inner' and 'outer' make sense only with reference to a mediating boundary that strives for stability . . . From what strategic position in the public discourse and for what reasons has the trope of interiority and the disjunctive binary of inner/outer taken hold?" (134). The interior/exterior metaphor better describes the sexual difference of lesbianism in psychoanalytic discourse than the male/female (or mother/infant) metaphor. Though Butler at this point was describing abjection as "the mode by which Others become shit" (134) as they are evacuated from an anxiously maintained interiority, that is also the point of revelation, where the Other becomes distinguishable (as shit).

Psychoanalysis seeks to bring out into the open what was hidden. Its revelations produce the "disjunctive binary" that makes the performance of revelation possible and help maintain an apparently safe insider's world that nevertheless can continue only through the repetitive performance of exclusions. The strategy of quarantining the lesbian object within the discourse that reveals her unconscious is essential to the production of theory that reaches its acme of authoritative coherence when its object is revealed as an abjected Other. This is the sexual difference of the lesbian in psychoanalytic theory. To maintain the boundary, it is only necessary to continue to express apprehensions about how the female homosexual fits into a heterosexual matrix and what her presence there might mean. However, the function of the lesbian as heterosexuality's abject, or as the neglected Other in feminist object relations, or as a potentially happy stopover on the way to heterosexuality, or as an ecstatic or pathetic attempt to return to the preoedipal mother does not preclude the possibility that there could be something important about lesbians that does not figure in (the margins of) psychoanalysis.

I broach this possibility of a *something else*, another way of configuring "lesbian," because I have found it difficult to locate my own experience in psychoanalytic theories about lesbians. I also found it difficult to locate my own desires and experiences in the only definition of "lesbian" I had access to when I was young. In those years just after Stonewall (though I heard nothing of that) and located in one of the more liberal parts of the United States, I learned that lesbians are sleazy, bitter, hard women who (ludicrously) believe they can take a man's place and so prey upon vulnerable women who cannot attract men. In its expression of bitterness and futility, as well as its portrayal of the lesbian as enacting a fiction, this frequent definition had much in common with early psychoanalytic theories that still persist in conservative psychoanalysis.[5] What I could have used then was not an elegant discussion of the fluidity of gender and sexuality, but practical and positive definitions, something useful for claiming an everyday experience of desire and countering the authoritative judgment that a lesbian lives out a pitiable imitation of desire she cannot have. I lived a private experience that I could neither articulate according to the then-authoritative definition nor use to refute it. However, the lack of a proper definition—that is to say, a phallic lack—could neither annul nor even dilute desire. Lacking authority is not the same as lacking agency.

I will use one other brief personal example to elaborate on the action of theoretical de-authorization. Years ago, in a casual conversation, a friend of mine claimed that penis envy is universal in the lives of women. "But," I objected, "I can't remember ever feeling penis envy." She reminded me that penis envy is operative even if it never reaches the conscious level or develops from a visual encounter with a penis; sexual difference structures our psyches whether we know it or not. Penis envy is only a metaphor that underwrites women's relation to the phallus. My denial served only to confirm my inability to accede to "the fact of [my] castration," however symbolic that castration might be (Freud 1953, 257). Bristling, I asked her why I could look around inside my own head forever and not find penis envy, while she could identify it unerringly.

It would be possible to argue about whether denying penis envy is a sign of a lesbian sexual difference, but what is important here is the way that users of theory—insiders—process resistance as support for theory. I tried to use my divergent personal experience to deauthorize universality in theory. The unconscious envy my friend attributed to me, however, is not personal. It is part of a universal feminine unconscious that conforms to conventional structures of heterosexual difference. The claim to universality maintains a protected insider's space personal experience such as mine cannot penetrate. If my consciousness remains mulishly disaffected from the feminine unconscious, my understanding has no authority to speak. What I could not say authoritatively can, however, emerge within the insider discourse, as it did in a press release from the American Psychoanalytic Association that declared, "Penis Envy? Freudian Psychoanalysts in the 90's Say, It Ain't Necessarily So!!!"[6] Until the "personal" can speak its own authority, attacking universalism and its more biologically directed corollary "essentialism" on their own ground will not succeed.

A public and far more advanced theoretical disagreement on psychoanalysis demonstrates how heterosexual authority constructs and maintains a sense of who belongs on the inside and who must be rejected—or abjected—in the interests of theoretical purity. Molly Anne Rothenberg and Joseph Valente (1996) accused Diana Fuss (1992) (no novice to psychoanalytic theory) of proposing the unthinkable in "Fashion and the Homospectatorial Look": that somewhere in the female heterosexual unconscious a lesbian lurks, latent until excited by erotically charged images of women that a heterosexual woman would presumably identify with rather than desire. The divide between identification and desire is based on conventional assumptions of the meaning of sexual difference: as there is no difference between women, they must not desire one another. Fuss critiqued her own article for being "far too uncritical of the discourse from which it sprang," but I continue to like her reading of the "lesbian vampire" as a figure through which one might understand how "heterosexuality secures its identity by at once disavowing and perpetually calling attention to its abject, interiorized, and ghostly other, homosexuality" (1996, 383).

Heterosexuality can maintain its identity as the dominant sexuality only as long the heterosexual female's experience of identification cannot be seen to involve something like a sexual desire-to-have. Fuss's "homospectatorial look" had no place in Rothenberg and Valente's schema because heterosexuality cannot function as such without assimilating the idea of homosexuality to itself. In this case, assimilation means suppressing the proposition that the other could have an identity the assimilator has not named and contained. Suppressing this proposition means that the idea of homosexuality can serve as a resource for heterosexual fantasy and identity. The assertion that the heterosexual woman has no inner lesbian and that she lacks a desiring homospectatorial gaze is a way of assimilating the idea of homosexuality to formulate a heterosexual perspective. Thus, when Rothenberg and Valente accused Fuss of unwittingly theorizing that "lesbianism stands in an imperialist relation to heterosexual women," they performed the colonizing gesture they claim Fuss cannot, with the bonus of heterosexual privilege to back them up (1996, 382).

Rothenberg and Valente amplified their efforts to suppress Fuss by asserting that any attempt to account for any identity is essentialist. To support their claim, they cite Walter Benn Michaels (1992), who argued regarding race that antiessentialism required "ceasing to explain what people do or should do by reference to who they are and/or what culture they belong to" (376n. 3). This would make it impossible to differentiate according to membership in a particular group because that would involve producing an account of identity, an essentialist act. Applied to the realm of sexual difference, this is advantageous for heterosexuality, which—as the unmarked and dominant sexuality—has no need to explain or justify its behaviors. Rothenberg and Valente wielded this antiessentialism to deprive lesbianism of so much as a toehold in theoretical space. If it is always essentialist to posit any (lesbian) identity, there is no way for lesbians to mark their sexuality, recognize each other, bring about desire, establish coalitions or communities, or speak of their existence.[7] Though made ostensibly in the interests of acknowledging that "gender, race and so on are never fixed by any stable set of cultural forces," Rothenberg and Valente's accusation of "profound essentialism" seems less like a demand for rigor and more an attempt to muzzle a theorist. No matter how "finely [Fuss] calibrates the relevant background factors and their operation," any generalization she might make about the mechanisms of identification rendered her argument essentialist and therefore null (377).

In her response, Fuss pointed out Rothenberg and Valente's unacknowledged position and describes its effects; their "omission is not, of course, mere oversight: the use of an objective, moralizing, and universal voice is one of the standard tropes of homophobic discourse" (1996, 383). By using this voice, Fuss argued, "the authors take this lesbian theorist to task for willfully refusing to get it straight" (1996, 387). She further argued that Rothenberg and Valente's essay "is not an argument *with* lesbian theory but an argument *over* it, a defiant and hostile challenge to the very idea of lesbian theory as such" (385).

Although the issue of the moment is what might become of lesbian sexual difference as it informs patterns of identification and desire, there remains the more basic problem of how to establish a space in psychoanalytic discourse in which interested parties might speak with each other. I am not (and Fuss certainly did not) advocating the use of identity politics in a vain attempt to establish impermeable walls between heterosexual and lesbian theory, but lesbian theory cannot evolve under the authority of unacknowledged heterosexual privilege.

Sexual Difference, Unauthorized

> In order to prove the applicability of the symbolism of psycho-analysis, it would be necessary to show that a symbolic interpretation from other entirely different points of view would not be equally plausible.
>
> —Franz Boas

Jacqueline Rose (1989) proposed to replace an illusory and oppressive dualism with sophisticated, flexible, and complex conceptions. She wrote: "I want to suggest that feminism, precisely through its vexed and complex relationship with psychoanalysis, may be in a privileged position to [refuse] the rigid polarity of inside and outside together with the absolute and fixed image of sexual difference which comes with it and on which it so often seems to rely" (28). The good news is that heterosexual difference could present a more flexible, expansive, depolarized image as it evolves in response to feminism's "vexed and complex relationship with psychoanalysis." But I am not convinced that this new heterosexual difference will abandon the authoritative strategies of the more established versions. The old heterosexual difference persists not only as a historical necessity underpinning the feminist evolution. It is alive in the new (de)constructions, where it continues to structure the inner and outer space through which the new heterosexual difference moves, blurring distinctions and proliferating parts.

Suspecting that the best way to address the issues is to grapple with them experientially, I propose a thought experiment, an alternative reading of the meanings of heterosexual difference from a lesbian point of view. I am not sure if what follows contributes to or works against the possibilities for a new, more flexible heterosexual difference, but with my alternative reading as a counterpoint and guide, I will elaborate a few of the problems I believe persist in theories about sexual difference and the development of women's sexuality. The problems I will analyze affect the content of theory, but they do not originate there. They are produced, rather, in the process of building theory, as a response to the social and intellectual structures that determine what is thinkable. Because establishing the authority to speak is crucial to building theory, I will use and then critique two strategies that help accomplish that task: (1) reiterating and revising conventional forms, and (2) repressing the personal in the service of the universal.

In describing some of the misunderstandings that affected the early development of psychoanalytic theory, Freud remarked that the child "does not begin its sexual investigation with the problem of sex differentiation and is far from entertaining the social under valuation of the woman. There are women in whose neurosis the wish to be a man never played any part" (1917, 47). Keeping in mind Freud's comments about what the child does not do and the wish a woman may not have, I intend to think about "lack" from the perspective of a peculiar child who learns to experience her sex not as a nothing-to-be-seen but as a space for initiating pleasurable and useful distinctions. My thinking has its origins in an early and persistent refusal to accept certain aspects of heterosexual difference that structured the world in which I moved. This account is not autobiographical, but is a patchwork of evidence gleaned from conversations with women of various orientations. If it differs from accepted accounts, that difference is in the evidence I feel compelled to pay attention to.

The problem I plan to address can only be stated as a question for which I will find no resolution: How does a girl create meaning from the fact of heterosexual difference? All that can be stated with certainty is that the little girl believes in the first instance that all human beings have genitals like hers. From this solid first point, however, it is possible to locate a few points along the developmental road where careful observation connects overt behavior and perception on the one hand with unconscious processes on the other.

Let us begin with a little girl of four who inadvertently witnesses her older brother emerging from the shower. She suffers a shock when she sees her brother's genitals. The intensity of her response is no less profound because he hurries to cover himself. In a flash she constructs a theory to account for their difference: parts meant to be inside his body had fallen out. For her this represents the possibility of a fearful calamity. The first sight of male genitals initiates a process for which no proper metaphor can be found within the body of classical myth. We may call this the incontinence complex.

The girl's genitals now begin to assume a central role in her self-image. It occurs to her that they are compact and perfect, an impression much enhanced by the powerfully pleasurable sensations her genitals are capable of producing. It dawns on the girl that boys are incapable of feeling or functioning as she does. Could the catastrophe boys suffer happen to her? Perhaps this is a punishment to which she might be subject as well. She wonders if those parts could be put back. She realizes that her father must also have suffered this calamity, and she cleaves to her mother for affirmation that she will remain intact. She muses that men wear clothes to conceal their physical deformity and women wear clothes so that the men won't feel envious. She tries to emulate her mother, treating her father and brother with the condescension and exaggerated care associated with femininity. That men seem to enjoy this and fail to perceive the settled contempt that underlies her condescension confirms her theory that males are substandard. A feminine stance, whatever its vicissitudes, helps to distinguish her from men and reassures her of her superiority. Thus the context is created that encourages the girl to develop a heterosexual orientation, which, deriving as it does from guilt about her own intactness and her striving to maintain that intactness by identifying with her mother's strength, begins to mediate between unconscious and conscious levels of thought. If, alternatively, the ambivalent satisfactions of the heterosexual pattern are not enough to sustain her erotic and emotional interest, she may develop a female homosexual or bisexual orientation.

If her father is the disciplinarian, the girl's attachment to her mother will be fueled by her belief that her mother avoided the incontinence that afflicts boys and might be able to protect her from her father's revenge. If her mother is the disciplinarian, the motivation differs, but the result is the same. She will continue to attach herself primarily to her mother and will defer to her authority, to avoid the punishment men have already undergone, perhaps at the hands of angry mothers. The girl may worry about it occasionally, but the incontinence complex does its work in the unconscious. The girl's knowledge of male deformity continues to feed her sense of superiority until the growth of breasts, which many girls despise at first, recognizing in them a masculine excess. The conflicts that arise during puberty in response to profound changes in both form and functioning of the body may be evidenced later in life in women's conflicted or muted experience of sexual desire, but this can be mitigated where there is a history of strong maternal attachment and identification. A deep attachment to the mother permits the girl to weather puberty with a healthy sense of bodily and psychic integrity. Meanwhile, the dismissive, tolerant, loving, or angry things she hears her mother and her mother's women friends say about men begin to take on a deeper meaning.

Reflecting on encounters with women's barely concealed or blatant distaste for and/or pity of men, their expressions of guilt, their enduring frustration and disappointment with their husbands' inability to connect with them emotionally or sexually, their rage and shame, endurance and resistance in the face of domestic violence, their internal conflicts over whether men deserve to have a greater share of money, food, decision-making power, leisure, luxury, and security, their difficulties in providing material and emotional support for other females in families and institutions, their assumption that women bear the principle responsibility for maintaining family relationships, their calling each other to account for perceived violations of women's "natural" need to nurture, their myriad attempts to repair wounded male pride, and injuries for which they often feel unaccountably responsible—in view of all this, it is hardly possible to avoid the conclusion that an incontinence complex directs feminine development. For most women, these deeply buried impressions linger, surfacing unbidden in the fleeting realization that there is something uneconomical and excessive about being male.

It is also not surprising that women's internal conflicts sometimes erupt in a desire to castrate men, expressed either in fantasy or reality. What underlies this hostility is an equally powerful impulse to resolve the problem of masculine incontinence on a symbolic level or, in infantile terms, to put back the fallen organs. Only a powerful internal censor, developed out of the incontinence complex, prevents enactment. The degree to which women keep a firm lid on their rage can be appreciated by considering the intense public response to Lorena Bobbitt, who cut off her husband's penis, helped locate the missing organ, and then reestablished a relationship with him. Incidences of such maiming remains small, so many fewer than the number of male-on-female rapes and maimings that they cannot be accounted for statistically.[8] *This indicates that women have been far more successful in working through the incontinence complex than men have been in working through the castration complex.*

The impulse to castrate men as a compensation for men's excessive violence or greed illustrates the most disturbing as well as the most deeply buried aspect of the incontinence complex. However, its positive central feature, the desire to repair the male organs, must already be present in the little girl even if she does not experience sexual abuse by males. If it is possible for a little girl to respond with pity and distaste rather than envy to her first view of the male genital apparatus, and on the basis of that response construct a theory in which being a boy is a liability, what are the implications? On the basis of her theory, she can establish the dual cause of male privilege as men's fragility and women's support. If her brother is clearly the favored one—if her parents pay greater attention to his problems and praise him lavishly for small achievements—the girl would conclude that, fit and self-sufficient as she is, she is not in need of similar pampering and neither are other girls. In sum, she is grateful for being female and hopes fervently that no accident befalls her like the one that damaged her brother, but she views being a woman as a heavy responsibility. This view creates enduring conflicts between the hope that she will be able to meet the responsibilities of womanhood and the resistance based on the perhaps unconscious knowledge that if she meets all expectations, she will have lived her life in the service of an inferior dependent. The girl's childish theory serves her self-image, and if she can retain her own sense of being well made while granting that neither women's nor men's lives are determined by their genitalia, she will free herself of many of these conflicts. Time and experience must, however, present numerous challenges to her confidence, especially if the care she gives others is not reciprocated.

It is significant that feminism emerges as the first historically determined solution to the incontinence complex. The budding feminist frees herself from the misperception that the excess represented in male anatomy must find its inevitable corollary in men's expectation—deriving from their own infantile fear of personal inferiority—that they should command excessive power in the family and in institutions. Thus feminism, expressed in women's demands for equal access to education and the professions, the personal control of reproduction, and an end to male violence against women can be seen for what it comprises: a rejection of male excesses and a demand for equality that has its basis in the transformative effects of the incontinence complex. The feminist enjoys an attitude of respect for self and (male) other that frees her of the old illusion that men's self-images are too fragile to survive without constant support.

Authorizing Uncertainty

The girl's personal theory of sexual difference helps her negotiate the specific material and psychological complexities of growing up female in her world, but as a universal theory it will not work. In fact, the theory of the "incontinence complex" contains some egregious errors. I have not accounted for a range of developmental paths that might look radically different. I have not brought up evidence that runs counter to the account I've sketched. I have not suggested cross-cultural differences or even given "the girl" any markers that would align her with a racial group, religion, or class. "The girl," therefore, is white, Christian, and middle class by default. I have permitted the pretense that a roughly middle-class liberal feminism is the only feminism. What makes it bad theory, then, is not its argument, but the omissions that its structure and its genealogy encourage.

This speculation could be reinterpreted to support a traditional psychoanalytic account of feminine development. In spite of its deviance, the girl's primary encounter with heterosexual difference leaves in place virtually all of the terms and blank spaces of more conventional psychoanalytic accounts. Heterosexual difference is still preeminent, for it inaugurates her (illusory) self-concept, constructing a subject-in-crisis that even at the best of times will be under threat of dissolution. The girl will find it hard to move beyond the binary logic that produces this threat. Except for the deviant understanding resulting from her first encounter with the distinction between the sexes, the girl is unremarkable.

Another problem with this account is its unacknowledged proposition: not "there is sex in everything" but "when it comes to women, sex is all there is." The first proposition admits the ubiquitous influence of sexual difference; the second might explain Freud's reluctance to define a woman by anything other than her sexual function. The "case" of the girl's encounter with heterosexual difference, even if it is deviant in some ways, is no more key to the girl's sense of self than many other moments that would fail to attract the attention of a theorist on women's development. How does the girl's world shift when, for the first time, a black classmate enters her all-white classroom and becomes her seatmate under the disapproving eyes of her teacher? How is her self-concept shaped when her family fortunes change suddenly and she finds herself living in a trailer without toilet or running water? How does she recover from the grief of losing her best friend to a "born again" Christian sect? The relation between these experiences and the unfolding of heterosexual difference is not a relation between the particular and personal on the one hand and the universal on the other. Heterosexual difference cannot hold steady as a theoretical concept against the influence of other ways of knowing because it does not precede them and cannot be abstracted from them. But what this girl might do, if she existed and were authorized to speak for herself, is suggest that there is more to be learned from ruminating for a very long time on the differences among women than from the practice of reiterating and reforming ideas about the meaning of heterosexual difference.

If it is possible to imagine that the conventions by which theorists establish authority may encourage the creation of accounts that distort rather than yield an accurate understanding of an individual, then the question of who benefits is especially urgent. Barbara Christian posed this problem in relation to African American women's literature in which self-definition is a tool of survival: "If they tried to live by the female version of The American Dream, as pure, refined, protected, and well-provided for, they were often destroyed" (1993, 318). One derives no benefit from investing in universal models when experience drives home the realization that you are betraying your own interests.

By "interests" I do not mean only social and political welfare, but also intellectual concerns. A successful provisional theory about some women's development would arise in order to address a specific situation, locatable in time and space. It would acknowledge complexities that might disrupt it. Its originators would implicate themselves openly in its applications, and refrain from making obsessive appeals to an authoritative origin. They would decline to exercise their unearned entitlement to name the experience of a theoretical object.

Anne Phillips (1992), addressing the issue of universalism in political thought, indicated that "the mistake of much conventional theory has been to see this process as one of delving behind the insignificant differences of being to come up with a purified core" (27). The descriptive power of universal theories is limited in precisely the ways that allow them to serve those whose interests are invested in an unmarked, abstract being—the white, heterosexual, and middle-class person—who occupies the category "normal." Phillips's desire to see theorists begin to pay attention to information they previously thought insignificant was a desire to see them divest themselves of privilege. It is difficult to imagine what—beyond a revolution or an extraordinary degree of insight and altruism—would cause them to accede.

Conventional theory lacks the imaginative space within which to experience its own limits. That lack is evident in Nancy Chodorow's (1989) criticism of "unitary conceptions" of male and female in psychoanalysis. She charged that "psychoanalytic theories speak in global terms of 'the girl,' 'the boy,' 'the man,' 'the woman'" and argued, "we must understand gender as it relates to other identities and other situated aspects of social and cultural organization" (196). Chodorow attributed errors in psychoanalytic theory not to Freud but to his later adherents, and she argued that Freud's conception allowed for "a multitude of 'women'": "Freud's descriptions of women and of his interactions with them involve a large cast of characters, a pantheon of greater and lesser ideal-typical goddesses and mortals to complement and accompany Oedipus, Narcissus, Moses, and others into psychological glory or ignominy. We also find actual, historically specific, late nineteenth- and early twentieth-century named and nameless women in clinical cases and vignettes" (1994, 2). None of these women, including the "actual, historically specific" ones, are women in the world. They are female characters, goddesses, case studies, and types, known only through the evidence Freud saw fit to present. They existed to relate to the male figures they "complement and accompany."

In Chodorow's version of psychoanalytic theory, female figures were defined in connection, and heterosexual difference structured their relations. Feminine connection, which Chodorow considered an attribute of feminine personality, was a structuring device necessary to the production of her theory. As Chodorow (1994) expanded her conception of the multiplicity of women, she translated these figures into their mundane incarnations, writing that in Freud's work, "women are young girls, mothers of daughters and mothers of sons, daughters of mothers and daughters of fathers; they are heterosexual, lesbian, sexually inhibited or frigid altogether; they are substitute mothers as nursemaids, servants, or governesses; they are wives, mother-symbols, or whore-like sexual objects of desirous or fearful men" (3–4). The scope within which women can demonstrate the multiplicity Chodorow ascribed to them or envision what Chodorow calls "an I, who is female," is limited to the attributes that can be readily assimilated within her theoretical structure, but the fact that women's variability is limited here to differences of sexual and reproductive status is not, in itself, a problem (1994, 3). These differences are significant and complex, and the subtleties of women's evolving relation to heterosexual differences could occupy good minds for as long as there are women. The problem begins, as Chodorow asserted, with theories that claim to be "universal" and so avoid the rigorous exercise of identifying the limits of their descriptive power. The possibilities for defining "an I, who is female," in Chodorow's argument coincided with her own earlier assertions about feminine personality structures:

"Certain features of the mother-daughter relationship are internalized universally as basic elements of the feminine ego structure . . . In any given society, feminine personality comes to define itself in relation and connection to other people more than masculine personality does. (In psychoanalytic terms, women are less individuated than men are; they have more flexible ego boundaries.)" [1989, 45–46].

The structure of feminine personality fits in well with the authoritative conventions, but this capsule argument demonstrates how Chodorow appealed to feminist psychologists in the United States. The qualifiers "less" and "more" serve as a rhetorical hedge against the totalizing terms "universally," "basic," and "in any given." Feminine connection happens everywhere, for every woman, in every time, but it is only a tendency. The potential negativity of "less individuated" is offset by the positive term "flexible," ascribing to women a universal feminine trait that itself challenges "the absolute and fixed image of sexual difference" Rose (1989) identified as one of the main problems in psychoanalytic theory (28). Chodorow's theories were successful (i.e., they have become an enduring part of the psychoanalytic and feminist discourse) because the contradictions embedded in her thinking appeared to be efforts to bring concepts into balance. Confronting and elaborating on those contradictions would mean a loss of authority.

I do not, however, mean to imply that it is impossible to challenge and change the authoritative conventions. Rosi Braidotti (1989), arguing for a new feminist understanding of essentialism, found it "historically and politically urgent, in the *here and now* of the common world of women to bring about and act upon sexual difference" (100). Rita Felski (1997) interpreted Braidotti as making sexual difference "the prototype of all differences" (7).

If heterosexual difference is prototypical, it must be structurally stable, and the subject who refuses to recognize this stability cannot aspire to coherence. In her response to Felski, Braidotti corrected the misperception, writing, "sexual difference can be understood only in terms of multiple differences" including race and sexual orientation among others, a point that renders moot the question of whether sexual difference is or is not prototypical (1997, 27). According to Braidotti, what brings about and acts upon sexual difference is a "feminist cogito," an identity-thought more capable of taking action than Chodorow's "I, who is female." Braidotti's "I" was sexed, but the meaning of her sexual difference could not be fixed by naming her "woman": "The affirmation of my subjectivity need not give a propositional content to my sense of identity: I do not have to define the signifier woman in order to assert it as the speaking subject of my discourse" (1989, 100). Asserting the material existence of women over the bodiless and appropriable feminine, Braidotti invoked both the differences within a woman and the "differences *among* women: differences of class, race, and sexual preferences for which the signifier 'woman' is inadequate as a blanket term" (1989, 93).

This is an essentialism that enables political action, implying a collectivity, a "we" that can bring about social change, while barring the production of a monolithic or stable definition of "us." Braidotti's rethinking of the term "woman" could be used to stem the proliferation of charges of essentialism of the kind that Valente and Rothenberg brought against Fuss, but I am most interested in another promising effect of Braidotti's argument. If feminist theorists are fully occupied with trying to establish or refute authoritative definitions of "woman" (or "lesbian" or "sexual difference")—if, in other words, they are thinking too much about correctness and too little about usefulness—then the most they can accomplish is maintain a defensive screen around their discourse.

Desiring and Theorizing

Teresa de Lauretis's discussion of "sexual indifference" in *Practice of Love* (1994) demonstrated the effects of balancing concerns about usefulness and psychoanalytic correctness. According to de Lauretis, feminism's emphasis on male/female sexual difference obscured "the effects of other differences in women's psychosocial oppression," but its effects were also positive, for it created "a critical space—a conceptual, representational, and erotic space—in which women could address themselves to women" (5). Their negotiations settled nothing, but for de Lauretis, they helped to clarify other social contradictions: "It thus appears that 'sexual difference' is the term of a conceptual paradox corresponding to what is in effect a real contradiction in women's lives: the term, at once, of a sexual *difference* (women are, or want, something different from men) and of a sexual *indifference* (women are, or want the same as men). And it seems to me that the racist and class-biased practices legitimated in the notion of 'separate but equal' reveal a very similar paradox in the liberal ideology of pluralism, where social difference is also, at the same time, social indifference" (5).

The contradiction of "sexual indifference" is real for women, but it does not originate in and live out its life cycle within a closed system of feminine psychology, any more than "separate but equal" was the product of the mental and emotional dynamics of African Americans. Realizing this opens a critical space within which those Others not best served by indifference might develop theories more useful to them. The sexual indifference de Lauretis was most closely concerned with reduces lesbian sexuality to formulations such as "pre-Oedipal fusion, psychosis, hysteria, bisexuality, or oscillation between masculinity and femininity" (75). These metaphors accumulate as a concealing fog around practices that function like the truer statement about racial difference: separate and unequal.

In light of the discourses of sexual indifference, de Lauretis's claim that "it takes two women, not one, to make a lesbian" was both more radical and more ambiguous than the immediate implication that a lone woman will be perceived as heterosexual. On one hand, if it takes two women to make a lesbian, the equation reflects a lack of sexual difference, so that one plus one equals one (lesbian). It looks like fusion, the loss of individuality, overidentification, an autoerotic or narcissistic relation in which "love" is not for the other but for some alienated part of the self. Lacking an external object, lesbians break down subject/object distinctions and make desire impossible. This is how "sexual indifference" operates in its conventional mode.

On the other hand, if it takes two women to make a lesbian, then "lesbian" comes into being in some sort of sexual relation between individual women. Seeking precise distinctions between identification and desire, de Lauretis faulted Jackie Stacey for failing to articulate what differences fuel the desires Stacey thought erupted between women characters in the movie *Desperately Seeking Susan*. De Lauretis argued persuasively that the film is about identification (wanting to be, or to be like, the other woman), and not about desire (wanting to have the other woman). Like the conflict between Fuss and her critics around similar theoretical issues, this was more than a conflict about how a heterosexual woman relates to erotically charged images of women. Whereas Rothenberg and Valente were concerned about an imperialist lesbianism that, if it had any real power, would make it harder to see women as purely heterosexual, de Lauretis's intervention created a space for imagining a lesbian desire that cannot so easily be subsumed in the vision of a heterosexual woman aspiring to be like an image of woman that is sexually desirable to men.

De Lauretis's critique resisted the conventional operation of "sexual indifference" that configures any relation between women (heterosexual or lesbian) as solely an expression of identification. According to de Lauretis, identification and desire can coexist, but the relation "cannot be blithely taken for granted but must be articulated theoretically" (121). For de Lauretis, theoretical articulation could be best accomplished by examining "a complicated passage (in developmental terms) through Oedipal—phallic and genital—drives and such instinctual vicissitudes as sadomasochism, exhibitionism, voyeurism" (121).

At this point the search for a more accurate understanding of lesbian desire seems to arrive back at a point of sexual indifference. I am reluctant to follow the complicated passage de Lauretis proposed, mostly because it is difficult for me to imagine how and by what motivation perversion (as pathology or as a deviant relation to social norms) could be integrated into psychoanalytic theory without functioning as a site for repetitive performances of exclusions. In her review of *The Practice of Love*, Elizabeth Grosz (1997) wondered "what is at stake in trying to include what was previously excluded, to place at the center what was marginalized, to explain and analyze what was inexplicable and unanalyzable?" (296). In her response to Grosz, de Lauretis (1997) described the book as a "wild attempt to map a space between heterogeneous theoretical domains . . . to account for a kind of desire that I have lived in the terms of a conceptual universe, that of Freud's psychoanalysis, in which it is not understood or contemplated but through which I nevertheless think" (325). The answer to Grosz's question—what is at stake?—was perhaps the ironic experience of negotiating a space for a theoretically excluded lesbian desire within a theoretical system that could not exist in its present form if it could be made to integrate effective accounts of lesbian desire. The debates about identification and desire are unlikely to establish stable distinctions between heterosexual and lesbian women, and even less likely to bring the prodigal lesbian back into the fold, but they may nevertheless be a starting point for understanding lesbian desire as something other than the container for what must be excluded within psychoanalysis.

It is possible to imagine that in the difference between "wanting to be" and "wanting to be like" a fractional but negotiable space opens up akin to the distinction between metaphor and simile, an opening also reflected in the oedipal shift from wanting to have the mother to wanting to have someone *like* the mother. Yet more room opens up in the difference between "wanting to be like" the other woman and taking pleasure in perceived similarities. Identification, not as a totalitarian enterprise but as a flexible alliance, might cooperate with desire. If an absolute distinction between identification and desire does not prevail, lesbians are as likely to be free agents as helpless victims of psychological cause-and-effect. Therefore, lesbian lovers are not required to supply some phallic substitute for heterosexual difference in order to establish a degree of separation in order to experience desire (though nothing would stop them from doing so). Nor are they required to diminish identification in order to regain a sense of their respective individuality in order to avoid "fusion."

I framed this argument in terms of what is *not* universally true for lesbians rather than in terms of what is true for lesbians because I find it difficult to identify characteristics shared among all women who claim the name "lesbian" for themselves. Cheryl Clarke, who has done much to bring black lesbian literature out into the open, entered the discourse via a series of breaches in public space: she attended a conference where black lesbians made themselves visible, read black women's fiction and poetry, confronted homophobic rejections of the writings of black gay men and lesbians, and heard women speaking out in open rebellion. Along with openings, however, come closures. The search for "authentic portrayals" of black lesbians makes it possible to interrogate images of black lesbians in the writings of white women and black men. At the same time, it privileges authenticity for its own sake, as if a writer can only claim the authority to characterize "the black lesbian" via an appeal to an idealized core identity. Thus, according to Clarke, Audre Lorde's *Zami* was "too mythic" and the lovers Shug and Celie in Alice Walker's *The Color Purple* were "too unselfconscious" (1993, 220). In sum, they flunked a racial and sexual authenticity test that is applied only to those who represent a marginalized experience and identity. Further, the distinction between what is authentic (inside) and inauthentic (outside) is meaningful only if it is a measure of intrinsic worth, a dubious essence that appears and disappears depending on where one stands in relation to the object under judgment. Moving, at least for a moment, out of the place of judgment allows one to see another kind of knowledge taking shape. Lorde and Walker (and Clarke as well in her poetry) expanded the range of what is imaginable by seizing the space that opens when conventional assumptions fail and using it to imagine a black lesbian making her own myth and loving women unselfconsciously.

If the conventional assumptions are incorrect—if sexual and racial (in) difference need not define lesbian relationships—then how else can we articulate the differences through which identification and desire operate between and among women? And what if "difference" is more than a mechanism for the operation of desire and identification? Once acknowledged, difference proliferates beyond the binary models that accommodate sexual and social indifference, forming complex networks and building upon interrelationships in which formerly preeminent distinctions lose their authority to determine reality. From there, there is no way back to any basic, irreducible sexual difference.

Both de Lauretis and Braidotti were trying to free concepts that authoritative discourses have assimilated. If "woman" only means one thing, if she is fixed in a particular meaning by the structure of heterosexual difference, even if she is fixed in the category marked "flexible ego boundaries" or "site of difference," then there is only one woman to deal with. If there is only one woman, there can be no lesbians and no meaningful discourse among women. Women can speak to men about their differences in order to negotiate a heterosexual relation but will have nothing of consequence to say to one another. Dissociating propositional content from subjectivity means that it is possible to speak "as a woman" and even "as a lesbian" to other women without occupying a prescribed place in a predetermined structure of heterosexual difference.

Making space

Observing the act of creation is the most promising method I can imagine for helping to make the "theoretical space" that more conventional accounts tend to foreclose. In "The Naked Majesty of God," Caroline Halliday (1990) followed a thematic and formal thread through some poems concerned with the dangers of being lesbian lovers and representing lesbian desire. "Lesbians go in and out" through an atmosphere of danger and suppression, "and our loving has to find a space within it" (80). In her own poetry, Halliday witnessed a point where lesbian eroticism was "outside safety, and outside limitations, into the wild places, both of our own experience, and of the street" (80). Cheryl Clarke's poem "Space Invocation," quoted as an epigraph for this chapter, did not find space but made it by naming its passages into the erotic body: "I must get to those spaces: / black space of throathole / brown space of asshole / red space of cunthole / sex space of no turning back" (1993, 8). In opening up those spaces, going through those "holes," one risks everything, but the alternative is unthinkable: no space, nowhere to desire or speak for oneself. Clarke's poem "Living as a Lesbian Underground, ii" mapped the unlawful space opened up at the juncture of language and eroticism. The first stanza reads:

> A faggot historian friend—once noted
> now hunted—smuggled me the latest
> in dyke fiction from Fiji.
> I had to eat the manuscript
> before I could finish it.
>
> (1993, 9)

Incorporating the text, making it part of the body's interior, was the only way to save the unfinished manuscript and its underground reader. The lines produced a discursive sexual difference that did not build itself out of male/female differences; the faggot historian friend recognized her desire without figuring himself as its object. Sexual difference arose instead in the distinction between being "noted" and "hunted" and in creating makeshift hiding places for the outsider in a world where insiders have claimed all for themselves.

The difference is that, within the space of the poem, an outlaw can have her desire (or at least eat it). Similarly, the "tasty piece of interracial erotica" the poet rescued in "Living as a Lesbian Underground" was about making space in the body for insubordinate sexual possibilities. In this turbulent intermediary text, the poet is on the run, trying to prevent her journal from being either stolen or censored. She finally gave it away verbatim on the street (but without revealing its contents to the reader of the poem). The making of word space and sex space occupied the end of the poem, as the poet wrote a prohibited word "over and over" but did not permit the word to slip into the text:

I recited it every time I wrote it.
Played with my sex
as I wrote it
over and over.
and said it as I came
over and over.

(1993, 13)

Like the dyke fiction at the beginning of the poem, the single unspeakable word at the end was both salvaged and lost. If it was to make space for coming, it could not be given out, even to those who might need it most. That is how an underground conception survives oppression, distortion, and displacement at the hands of insiders—those who claim to be able to name the experience of outsiders. I see Clarke's poetry as a guide for making theory about a lesbian sexual difference. The persistent invocation of space—the space of a word, the spaces of the sexual body—is also a persistent refusal to name a unitary or universal content for those spaces. Suspending "propositional content" makes space for one who desires, a subject, a speaker, without dictating identity.

On the effects of identity politics, I agree with Gwendolyn Bikis, whose story "Cleo's Back" I discuss below. In her author's blurb, Bikis (1999) wrote, "My work first appeared in lesbian publications in 1987; since then I have anticipated the day when identity politics is no longer lesbian fiction's main paradigm" (258). Identity politics has been useful in creating a space for writing by lesbians, but the paradigm that opens space also determines what can be said within it. Bikis' story, like Clarke's poetry, worked to make a space within which a wild subject—someone not already determined by her sex—could live out her desires.

"Cleo's Back" (1999) is one of a series of short stories Bikis wrote about Cleo: In this one, Cleo was getting out of prison. The narrator—not Cleo herself but Tammy, the woman who desired her—had "never, ever been 'inside,'" but she had heard what it is like from her sister Marla, who visited Cleo in prison and described "each dark corridor, each endless wait on a hard plastic chair in a crowded room where orders were orders and people were owned by crackers once more" (40). Not going inside the place where whites have a stranglehold on people and meaning enabled Tammy to dream of touching Cleo: "My fingertips itches to be pulling at her soft-napped hair, digging deep into it" (41). But if she could have her desire by refusing to enter the prison, it would be harder for her to hold out against her sister Marla: "But of course Marla, she won't see none of my longing—

not as long as Cleo's gone. Long as Cleo's gone, I still can hide it" (41). Marla liked to be in control and would do her best to keep Tammy from living out her desire for Cleo. At this moment, hiding it meant having it. When at last they were driving Cleo away from the prison, Tammy could not speak her longing, so she brought out a box of Good and Plenty.

> 'Member those first kisses you gave me? I am asking with my smile. 'Member their spicy taste of sweet black licorice? What I mean to be my meaning, without Marla getting in the middle, is that I want those Cleo kisses back. "Got some candy for you, Cleo," I say, and open up the box to pour some in her hand.
>
> Cleo grins down at her palmful of pink and white sweet pellets, and puts them in her mouth—all of them at once—and chews. "Mmm," she say, and grins, but she is looking at my thighs. "I likes Good 'n Juicy candy too," she whispers in my ear, while Marla's too intent on checking her rear blind spot and changing lanes to notice us too closely. (50)

The effort to say without saying, to make an inside language out of words and gestures that Marla could not prohibit, was for the moment the whole of their lovemaking. Not until Marla was called away for the evening could Tammy get Cleo into the room she had made into a home space. There Cleo began to free herself of the "inside" and Tammy freed herself of the "lonely midnight bed" she occupied while Cleo was away. As they made love Tammy decided to tell Marla everything, out of gratitude for "getting Cleo back for me" and because "everyone at home has always, in *all*ways, loved me" (56). This expansion of space, the decision to give out news of their love and lust, arose as she realized that what she and Cleo had at that moment was possible because of everything her family had given her.

When I try to imagine the result of using any of the most common psychoanalytic strategies to interpret Bikis's story or Clarke's poetry, I can only imagine a tortuous and distorted interpretation, a theoretical version of what the warrior poet in "Living as a Lesbian Underground" was up against. I have my own reasons for declining to see evidence of "pre-Oedipal fusion, psychosis, hysteria, bisexuality, or oscillation between masculinity and femininity" in these texts by Clarke and Bikis (de Lauretis 1994, 75). I take their texts as (also) theoretical, knowing that this reading puts into question what kinds of discourses can count as theory and moves into conceptual spaces that my own "unauthorized account" of sexual difference cannot enter. The conceptual space opening up in these texts cannot represent my experience or the contents of my unconscious, but the desire they allow for is familiar to me in all its fugitive brilliance. As a white woman living out an uneasy relation to the "crackers" whose practice it is to try to own people and meaning, I am again in a liminal space, a sexual insider and a racial outsider. From this position, the risk of attempting to go inside a text on the arm of an exclusionary theoretical discourse is too great.[9] What needs emphasis instead is the proposition that a dialogue with the "woman who may be a human being in other respects" will produce much that cannot be contained within the most influential theories available now, so many decades after Freud advised his audience to "enquire from your own experiences of life, or turn to the poets" for answers (1933, 135). At this historical moment, invoking space, creating a dialogue rather than a partition between those who get it and those who don't, listening for that part of experience or poetry that exceeds the theory, is the most promising strategy.

Conclusion: Queer Girl on Shaky Ground

> We have been sexually neutered by queer theorists, and baby-boomed into a classification of same-sex "couples" by sociologists. We emulate heterosexual marriages with commitment ceremonies, and we join the patriarchal army. Lesbians are in danger of vanishing . . . if we do not consciously create our own worlds.
>
> —J. Stelboum

> In a multitude of domains across the general cultural field, majority bodies are busy becoming lesbian.
>
> —C. Griggers

The afterlife

The golden age of lesbians is ending, or has ended, or might be about to end. Lesbian sexuality, colonized alike by pornographers and right-wing ideologues; lesbian love, co-opted into formal commitment; even the lesbian body itself, pressed into reproductive service and made to caricature heterosexual conventions—all that was lesbian vanishes unless we resist, and right now.

The call to arms is one side of postlesbianism. Another side is right-wing anti-lesbianism, which seeks to return us all to another sort of golden age in which no lesbians or other categorical perverts exist. Butler's (2004) account of the bracketing and then disappearance of "lesbian" from the language of various documents that resulted from the 1995 United Nations Meeting on the Status of Women describes one step in that direction

(2004, 181).[1] And finally there is the postlesbianism I identify as "queer," which seeks to deliver us to a utopian future in which no lesbians are needed and perversity circulates freely. The queer future may have ended already, or be about to end; if so, then it has earned its place right here in the conclusion.[2]

All of these worlds are fictions, and yet they reach out regularly and fiddle with reality. The most widely recognized recent antigay and antilesbian legislation, California's Proposition 8 (which bans same-sex marriage), means nothing outside the context of the various other worlds it is intended to create or prevent—a world in which religion, government, and society gather as a unified moral force behind an ideal vision of male-female union and the rights that vision promises, and another world in which same-sex couples partake of both the sentiment and the rights. Along with the true believers and the opportunists, there are also those who want to act fairly, on principle. What everyone involved shares is the ability to formulate at least an implicit sense of another world in wait, a world that must be forestalled or returned to or pushed forward.

I have offended some by asserting that in this way at least, science is not a special type of human phenomenon. I don't know of any sexual science that can justify the investment made in it except in that the results serve someone's nostalgic or optimistic or apocalyptic vision of what the world might become. That is true as much for the careful, objective, insightful study as it is for enterprises so marred by pretension and ideology that they should be shut down for shame. Having the sense of another world, implied or explicit, is not in itself a problem. The other world is an anchor, a knowable point that allows each of us, by means of a loose triangulation, to locate reality, determine our relation to it, and chart a course toward or away from some putative destination. The other necessary anchor point is supplied by whatever factual data we can access and are willing to consider relevant. This kind of other-worldly seeking is not divorced from the psychoanalytic kind of triangulation in which the child gains access to desire by using her parents as anchor points, but the problem with psychoanalysis is that it wants to come first and underlie everything that follows. I see the ability to formulate the sense of another world as basic to being human and psychoanalytic triangulation as just one use of that ability.

Depending on the results of one's calculations, that anticipated world might look like Jiménez's solidly heterosexual "shared reality"; Dörner's system of predictable hormonal switches; Socarides' and Sherfey's apocalyptic conceptions of unchecked sex and violence; Stoller's hopeful vision of starting over in a spirit of universal perversity; LeVay's anticipation of a world perfectly knowable through biological investigation; Welldon's universe of dangerous mothers; or any of the varied domains that can be plotted around burgeoning or reductive taxonomies of sex, sexuality, and gender. No matter where one tends, the sexual subject can certainly be found there, popping into view at the moment she escapes the lowered position of the pervert or the rat or strives for the elevated position of the theorist or researcher.

No matter where one starts or what end one seeks, the essential thing is to be able to chart a course toward a prospective world. With that in mind, and keeping an eye on the postlesbian, postfeminist afterworld that looms just over the horizon, I will look in on a course in queer theory I taught a few years ago under the aegis of a women's and gender studies program. The students were mostly privileged, left-of-liberal undergraduates who already knew something about postmodernism and were especially drawn to the notion of queer. Most favored affirmative action policies to produce racial equality. They could see the point of repealing laws that regulate sexual behavior, but they could not see any reason to favor legalizing same-sex marriage, promoting equality in adoption and custody proceedings, or supporting any law designed to protect the civil rights of lesbians and gays. "Lesbian and gay" (and, most particularly, "lesbian") seemed to them fictive identities, not real enough to stand up to queer theory's argument for the fluidity of sexuality, and therefore not real enough to merit political or legal representation. Racism, and to a much lesser degree sexism, were real oppressions of real groups of people, but homophobia was the dread of an illusory danger. "Homophobia" named an oppression directed at a person who was not really there.

The idea of a world where one could escape regulation by being unlocatable had a powerful appeal for these highly privileged students, some of whom spent their leisure time dumpster diving and their vacations in Europe traveling from one squat to another. It seems possible that people like these, for whom venturing somewhat outside the law and taking a leave of absence from affluence feel like exultant leaps into freedom, would find in the figure of the lesbian a peculiar appeal. It would seem that a lesbian, who can't even muster enough cultural representation to sponsor a fully fleshed stereotype, whose identity is so contestable that the typical oppressor can't even find her, would be a good candidate for their idea of queer. Surely no identity could be truly queer unless it approached the level of not-there-ness that marks "lesbian."

My students, however, were skeptical about the proposition that a person could be a lesbian and queer at the same time. "Gay" could be read as sexually free, risky on many levels at once, readably renegade, and therefore a candidate for queering. "Lesbian" seemed not just fictive, but old and obsolete. One would have to give up "lesbian" in order to join queer, which they thought of as a loose affiliation of sex-and-gender highfliers for whom identity categories are irrelevant. I suspected that for my students the rejected lesbian was racially specific but unmarked, and that guess turned out to be correct. "Lesbian" was generically white and European or American, and therefore lacking sufficient social currency in the context of the afterworld the students were imagining. However, they *could* imagine an African American or Palestinian lesbian as a person of queer consequence, because for them, "black" or "Palestinian" modify "lesbian" sufficiently to make the proposition negotiable, while "white" or "Jewish" are null.

There is a problem here, but the problem wasn't the students. When theory moves from the abstract to a more local context, it has to shed a great deal of its diplomatic ambiguity and get down to the business of demarcating boundaries—movable and subject to debate no doubt, but boundaries nonetheless. That necessity has especially ironic effects for queer theory, which was supposed to break down barriers between normal and abnormal, male and female (etc.). Who's in and who's out in the would-be queer world is determined by which identities arrive flush with social currency and which come with empty pockets. In other words, the queer world is ordinary. In my students' queer world, lesbians and feminists (and especially lesbian feminists) seemed sexually unadventurous if not prudish, ready to collaborate with conventional heterosexual norms, and worst of all racist—in sum, they lacked credit and were inadmissible.

The exclusion of lesbians and feminists is debatable, but the practice of defining by exclusion is so purely human—so ordinary—that it's essential. If "queer" let just anyone in, it would fail the people whose loves and lives and sexual behaviors have for so long made them the butt of derogatory terms like "queer." A universalized queer automatically atomizes to nothingness. No one can go there.

There is also a less apocalyptic reason to locate some boundaries: if anyone could enter the queer world just by eschewing allegiance to a specific sexed and gendered identity, then "queer" would be just another word for "liberal celebration of difference." Like the hegemony of white Anglo-Saxon Protestants in melting-pot America, which evacuated its old terms without otherwise transforming very much, there is nothing in queer theory to stop those who claim masculine identities from (re)asserting the authority masculinity has so readily commanded in other real contexts—and in future, fictive worlds as well. Some of those who are identified as female and feminine and therefore lacking authority in the pre-queer world have a better chance of asserting themselves in the queer world as men or as masculine women, or even as feminine people who refuse to take any macho guff, but none of those worthies can dismantle quantitative and hierarchical structures of sexuality and gender. Lesbians and/or feminists have met many such dead ends on the road to revolution, and their mulish inclination to point out the problems is, I believe, more troublesome to queer politics than their puritanism.

All this is a far cry from what Judith Butler (1993) was arguing for when she said she was permanently troubled by identity categories. Her desire to "have it permanently unclear what precisely" the term "lesbian" means when applied to her cannot be construed as a refusal to name the subject or a denial that the trouble "lesbian" generates can be meaningful and pleasurable, any more than her claim that she did not "understand the notion of theory" implied that she is not a theorist (308). For much of queer thought and practice, however, the trouble that "lesbian" represents is not central, useful, meaningful, or pleasurable. Instead, the term threatens to undermine queer theory's global reach, its promise of liberation, celebration of difference, and the fun of having sex.

Even those who find fault with queer theory sometimes fail to recognize its deep connections to feminism. In his concentrated critique of queer theory for its political apathy, I would have expected Max Kirsch (2000) to take up some feminist thought, especially considering his concern with social change. However, Kirsch failed to recognize how Judith Butler (for Kirsch the embodiment of queer theory) locates her work in relation to feminism, even though he began his chapter on performativity with this quote from Butler's *Gender Trouble*: "I began with the speculative question of whether feminist politics could do without a 'subject' in the category of women" (1990, 80). If he had considered Butler's connection with feminism, Kirsch would have had a chance to rethink his simple summation of feminism as "indebted to Enlightenment philosophies" (4).

Arguments in favor of biological essentialism, biological universalism, or a unified female subject are rare in feminism. Butler's question about whether feminist politics can do without a subject referred to an ongoing debate about how to define "woman" given "her" radical lack of unity, and the discussion had already reached a high level of sophistication when Butler wrote *Gender Trouble*. Rosi Braidotti, recommending a course that avoids both "nostalgic reappraisals of an authentic or essential 'human nature'" and the nihilism of "those who celebrate the implosion of sense, meaning and values for their own sake," sought instead to find out "how to recompose an ethical and political sense of agency of the subject" (389). The "sustainable self" that Braidotti derived from that middle course is not a politically impotent artifice but a matter of becoming. It endures as "a mobile entity in space and time" as it navigates "through sets of discontinuous variations, while remaining extraordinarily faithful to itself" (396).

The sustainable self has nothing to do with the terminally deconstructible subject that is the plaything of white, middle-class, male postmodernism. The postmodern subject functions as a more cynical version of the enlightenment subject whose fallibility and insubstantiality postmodernism delights in divulging. They are father and son, and both mark the place of an absent subject, one whose authority and social power work in the open but who cannot be held responsible. For instance, Jean Baudrillard (1990), a postmodern provocateur with an understanding of feminism no better than Kirsch's, claimed that women are all artifice: "here lies the secret of their [women's] strength which they are beginning to lose by setting up feminine depth against masculine depth" (133). The big advantage we are about to lose—that an attractive woman is powerful because her appearance entrances men—is one even an enlightenment subject would have been comfortable with. Whether masculine depth is a gratifying simulation (in the postmodern formulation) or man's real nature (in the enlightenment version), woman-as-surface works very well as his foil. Baudrillard recommended that women eschew feminism so that they could enjoy drawing men's attention to their feminine simulations. Another minor twist on the same idea was deployed as "fuck-me feminism" for a while in the early 1990s. Invoking old ideas about the meaning of femininity or appealing to liberal broad-mindedness are the kinds of strategies that make postmodern ideas and queer theory legible, indeed tolerable, for those who want to think big and change little.

For those who need big change, there is no ground to be gained by advocating for the terminally deconstructible subject. He exists as such only because he refuses to recognize women and queers as his peers. The sustainable self Braidotti described, however, is a familiar construction in feminist theory, and it appears also in queer theory, for instance, in the form of José Esteban Muñoz disidentified minoritarian subject (1999). It (or possibly "she") represents how our multiple and incommensurate differences belie holistic sisterhood, queer unity in difference, and the consumable "Other." Instead, the concept of the sustainable self offers a means of understanding how oppressed people search out the means of resistance proper to their context and goals.[3]

Rais Nur and A. R. (1994) contributed an essay to Monica Reinfelder's *Amazon to Zami* in which they spoke of the difficulties of forming a lesbian movement in Malaysia. They cited conservative religious beliefs, an oppressive regime, and legal proscriptions as the most significant problems. Their goal was to be public and political, but because they feared repercussions, they published under pseudonyms and did not acknowledge by name the lesbians whose experiences informed their essay. Among the wide array of obstacles to organizing a lesbian movement, they mentioned Malaysia's Internal Security Act (ISA), which allows for the detention of anyone the government sees as a threat to national security (78).[4] Their comments were prescient. In 1998, Anwar Ibrahim, the government minister who had been Prime Minister Mahathir Mohamad's presumed successor, was arrested under the ISA on politically motivated charges of sodomy and corruption. He was released in 2004.

Thus A. R. and Rais Nur's underground activism represented an ingenious response to treacherous political and social conditions. Unless one grasps the specific forms of regulation by gender and sexuality Malaysian lesbians are dealing with, their behaviors, including public silence, political apathy, anonymity, tendency to form tightly knit groups of friends, and the near universality of butch/femme relationships, are incomprehensible.

One of the indicators of the death of feminism is its assumed inability to describe how gender operates amid other essential aspects of social difference. In an early landmark essay, Gayle Rubin (1984) wrote that feminism developed the tools "to detect and analyze gender-based hierarchies," but could not "encompass the social organization of sexuality," so what was needed was a theory and politics that would do what feminism could not (170). The lesbian in all this occupied a kind of limbo. She might rent some space in feminism, but since she didn't concern herself with the question of how to be intimate with a man, she would always be an outsider within feminism. She would never be able to settle down in queer theory either. Her commitment to women—the "identity politics" of the lesbian feminist—spells out a set of strategies for resistance that allowed a few women to try to create sustainable selves in relation to the popularly recognizable categories of gender and sexuality. That's about all. It would hardly be reasonable to hope for more from any such figural identity.

Almost final propositions

When I started to think about the construction of recent history in queer, third-wave, and postfeminist thought, I was concerned that the search for final solutions to the problems of second-wave feminism and LGBT movements derived its fuel from unrecognized apocalyptic hopes unsettlingly similar to those that affect the right-wing psychoanalysis I discussed in chapter 2. That is to say, the end of the bad old world is announced, and the resulting carnage will be terrible but also satisfying. After all, being in the aftermath will mean not having to deal with whatever came before. It will be as if some parts of history had not been.

In this world, for instance, Audre Lorde cannot be seen as a lesbian and a participant in second-wave feminism. She can only be claimed as a third-wave icon and queer if she can be abstracted from her time and the discourses she helped shape. In this other world, Lorde's canonical open letter to Mary Daly is not an example of one lesbian and feminist calling another to account for her racism and failed scholarship, nor does it offer counsel to others who engage in feminist research and activism. Instead, it is a judgment on the unredeemable racism of the representative white lesbian/feminist who is (or rather was) the movement's sole proprietor. The bad lesbian and her cohort are uniformly unworthy, so their movement must give way.

Viewed from the perspective of those left behind, the queer new world is one of loss. Some radical lesbian activists, such as Alix Dobkin (2000), Lisa Vogel (2000), and Sheila Jeffreys (2003), interpreted the movement from butch to trans as postlesbian, an evacuation of lesbian identity and community. This interpretation, and the feelings of betrayal and grief that often accompany it, makes sense to those who define the limits of lesbian identity so narrowly that transgendered people don't have a place in the community. That definitional rigidity occasions some straightforward bigotry, but it derives from the fear of insignificance, of finding that one's claims of existence—always tenuous in the pre-queer world—are dissipating in a postmodern void.

The looming loss that the radical lesbians fear is manifest in some utopian elements of queer thought. An interviewee in *Off Our Backs* (Siegel

1993) saw in transgendered transformations the outlines of a great beyond: "Now, I will always be a feminist, regardless of the appearance of my body. I will always respect women. Transgender identity is one of the most radical revolutionary things people can experience. . . . I think it has the potential to carry us, to carry our community, to carry people beyond gender, beyond feminism, way into another place and it's incredibly exciting." A less elated and more academic "end of the world as we know it" statement concluded Zachary Nataf's (1996) brief exposition in *Lesbians Talk Transgender*: "The ongoing contestation and deconstruction of the monolithic gender system and the politicisation of the third gender category means that there will no longer be transsexuals and that lesbians as we know them will also cease to exist" (59).

The boundary queer theory constructs between the failed old and the promising new is the temporal counterpart of the division between binary gender and heterogeneous sex. The latter term in each pair refers to a free world beyond gender, lesbians, and (second-wave) feminism, while the first term refers to a world that is crumbling under the feet of the now-desperate lesbian/feminists, whose claim to theoretical and moral authority—to existence— is now as good as dead.

There is no way to know it in the new world, but trying to annihilate inconvenient female subjects is an old strategy that has never achieved better than partial success. Those pesky radical lesbian feminists keep banging on the queer door, demanding a hearing. When queer thought points to a postapocalyptic utopia without gender, for instance, it might want to listen to Sheila Jeffreys, who reports that radical lesbian feminism wants "to abolish what has been called 'gender' altogether"—not, however, to make way for the varied transgressions honored in queer theory and practice, but because she views those transgressions as nothing more than a means of obscuring the perfect synonymy of "masculinity" and "male-dominant behavior" (43). At a conference on the "lesbian postmodern" I listened as speaker after speaker remarked on Jeffreys's irrelevance. Why, I wondered, keep citing someone who makes no difference—who, under the terms I am using, appears not to be there? The reason is that Jeffreys is far from irrelevant. Her polemic is a sign posted as warning of where the queer thinker should not go: "here there be monsters."

What is monstrous is that she has a point. For instance, Jeffreys objected to using hormones to suppress the menarche of "Alex," a thirteen-year-old who had been born female but identified as male. Sounding like nothing so much as a dedicated queer, Jeffreys writes in reference to this case, "Feminists like myself envisage a time beyond gender when there is no correct way to behave according to body shape."[5] Good so far, but then she goes too far: "In such a world, it would not be possible to conceive of a gender identity clinic."

As long as we're imagining a world that might be, Jeffreys has logic on her side. In a world where gender doesn't matter, no one goes to any special effort to maintain, let alone change, gender.

The problem is that Alex doesn't live anywhere near a postgender world; he's making his way in this one, where gender identity clinics can be the gateway to a livable existence. Jeffreys's principal violation, the one that puts her beyond the pale, is not imagining a post-gender world; it is refusing to respect Alex's naming of his own gender. Refusing to respect the subject's self-naming is part of every act of oppression, and Jeffreys cannot follow that practice without hypocrisy.

In another sense, however, Jeffreys is making the same mistake as the queer theorists she denigrates. Those who gesture with revolutionary fervor toward a postgender or post-binary or post-male-dominated world cannot, as the old saw has it, get there from here. It is not possible to sustain the argument that the transgendered or butch subject offers a revolutionary promise more profound than the doubtful subject of feminism, "woman." Transgendered people do not and cannot move beyond gender; gender is the very ground they stand on. Instead, by crossing genders or refusing to adhere to rigid gender binaries, they make use of potentials for mobility and resistance that already exist in the gender system. Butler's statement that "man and masculine might just as easily signify a female body as a male one, and woman and feminine a male body as easily as a female one" perhaps overestimated the ease of signifying across conventional boundaries, but it also *under*estimated the elasticity of the existing signifiers, their availability for producing hybrids whenever and wherever the mainstream political environment permits (1990, 6).

The changed

Biddy Martin (1996) maintained that queer makes feminism the "fixed ground" against which it can appear to be antifoundationalist, performative, and playful (71–72). To illustrate her point, Martin turned to Eve Sedgwick, who, Martin says, perhaps unintentionally constructed gender, the female body, and procreation as the coarse material of feminism, and gay male sexuality as properly free from all that (76). This view reduces all of feminism to Jeffreys's vision, which featured a particularly rigid and judgmental regulatory system rooted in binary gender identity politics. Lesbians "become interesting," that is to say, they become subjects of theory and players in the queer world, when they break free of that system by identifying across genders.

At a meeting of the National Women's Studies Association some years ago, I attended a session titled "Is Trans the New Butch?" The queer promise of the title, the dynamic movement from one state to another, the whimsical reference to the world of women's fashions, are blighted by the quality of the implied relation between "butch" and "trans." Trans is the "new" butch; it represents progress, the ascendancy of one masculine gender identity over another. During the session, each story of personal transformation began with a statement that the speaker had always been a boy but had suffered from the degradation of being expected to be a girl. Their internal world was male and masculine, and only their skin-deep topography was female. One participant stated that the reward for leaving behind his false female identity was that now women treated him like a man. He knew he had made it when waitresses and clerks had begun to give him their "daddy's good little girl smiles."

Listening to these triumphant stories unfold, I hoped that someone among the speakers would challenge the rigidly polarized gender system in which the "butch to trans" subject created himself. I was hoping, in other words, for some of the critical thinking lesbian, feminist, and queer thought is supposed to make possible. Feminism in particular encourages women to believe that they are active, worthy of respect, powerful, and capable, so a feminist analysis might only serve to dampen his enjoyment of masculinity. The absence of feminism from the discussion suggested the validity of the Freudian idea that an allegiance to masculinity requires a repudiation of things associated with femaleness. The subject of "Is Trans the New Butch?" defined his gender identity in part by the absence of feminine characteristics and allegiances and in part by the assertion of masculine privilege.

There is an unproductive contradiction at work here, certainly not of Martin's making, that becomes most visible by taking the terms down to their crudest expression. The lesbian who can figure in the queer world is the one who, given the choice between allying herself with gender or sexuality, opts for the latter. However, she demonstrates her choice by identifying across genders, by "borrowing" or "stealing" or claiming to have always had the phallus, performing a gender ranging from butch to trans. Her sexuality emerges as fully queer when "she" becomes the wrong pronoun.

The contradiction that shows up in the figure of the lesbian crossing genders to get free of gender reflects an unresolved conflict of theoretical perspectives. Whenever the relation between feminism and queer theory is configured as a distinction between gender and sex, feminism is expected to play the woman, sticking to her conservative sphere, and queer theory plays the man, who can range as widely as he likes. This binds gender and sexuality together as if in a contentious but complementary heterosexual relation. Gender no longer determines sexual orientation or sexual behavior; but sexual agency, along with a host of privileges, is still understood to be masculine. The transgendered man or butch lesbian who identifies across genders is claiming his or her right to exercise sexual and social prerogatives feminine women are not supposed to have in their own right.

It doesn't work. Identifying across genders does not liberate one from gender regulation or to a freer sexuality. It means only that one identifies with a more privileged, favorable, comfortable, or personally fulfilling position in the system. It means receiving invitations to certain parties that one could not otherwise attend. Considered not as a monolith but as heterogeneous network, the sex/gender system can in some locations—those in which spiritual, sociocultural, and biomedical institutions are more open to variation—accommodate a great deal of instability and movement. In locations dominated by fundamentalism and moral codes determined by fear of contamination, the sex/gender system is rigid and punishing. Against the objection that cross-gender identifications entail uncomfortable and sometimes dangerous consequences, I would say that the social, economic, and personal risks involved in refusing to perform as the girl one is expected to be are not necessarily more profound than the risks of obedience. What matters is location. The rape and murder of Brandon Tina was a tragedy that carried a great deal of significance in queer communities and beyond, but feminine girls of about his age are also raped and murdered with alarming regularity by young men they know. Their deaths rarely make much of an impact beyond the circle of their friends and families because the risks women take in performing femininity are so ordinary they do not invite recognition or analysis—except among feminists.

The false assumption that a woman who appears to be feminine is safer and more likely to be accepted with respect is evident in Sherrie Inness and Michele Lloyd's essay on butch identity, "G.I. Joes in Barbie Land." They asserted quite properly (and queerly) that butch identity is independent of the direction of sexual desire. However, their butch attempts to make herself a radical outsider by refusing to have anything to do with femmes, and that, unfortunately, is not a valid passport out of existing sex/gender systems. Robin Maltz (1998) similarly took up the issue of butch "realness," but, speaking as a member of a stone butch/stone femme community, distinguished between mere butch lesbians who look "more like women than men" and stone butches, whose masculinity is so "real" that they can pass as male and heterosexual among the uninitiated (276). Even Judith Halberstam describes her elegant *Female Masculinity* as in part "an attempt to make my own female masculinity plausible, credible, and real" (19).

Dessert

> Thyme: If I can focus on something more specific, now, how do you like dildoes?
> Sky: Pleasure, hedonism, have nothing to do with gender.
>
> —T. Siegal, "Female To Male"

A few years ago, following Gay Pride in San Francisco, I went out to dinner with a group of lesbians. As soon as we were seated, the woman across from me remarked, "Look at that, femmes on one side and butches on the other." We were all wearing jeans and jackets. There were no remarkable differences in gender presentation that I could see, but it was important to this woman to have someone sitting on the "femme" side of the table to make her butchness real.

Having a woman try to assign a gender role to me so that she can reaffirm her masculinity doesn't feel much different from being used to guarantee a man's masculinity. This is true in spite of the fact that the woman's masculinity offends against patriarchal convention, while the man's masculinity and women's collaboration in reproducing it are his birthright. In both cases, I gather the "game" can be pleasurable as long as both parties take up their roles with some enthusiasm.

I studied femininity under the tutelage of my mother and grandmother. They taught me that femininity was a serious business that could keep me from poverty. My mother and grandmother looked at the social and economic evidence their own lives offered them and drew what seemed to be the logical conclusion: only under the protection of an economically viable man would any of us be able to build a livable life.

In spite of its emphasis on attracting a protector, this version of heterosexual femininity leaves no room for weakness or incompetence. Heterosexual convention expects a woman to locate in herself an essential femininity that makes the performance a pleasure for her, but to do it properly requires fusing one's solid body, so full of its own need, with such ephemera as false eyelashes and the right shade of pink lipstick. Outfitted thus, one embarks on a lifetime of daring performances, each of which disavows on its surface one's knowledge of the consequences of failure.

Another dinner. More lesbians. Over dessert, someone posed the question: when you look back at your life, what was the first clue that you were a lesbian? Each of the other women had a fond story from adolescence: one adored softball and idolized the gym teacher; another preferred to play with boys and thought girls were dumb; another hated dresses and managed by bullheaded resistance to wear her overalls every day, even to church.

I didn't have any such story of gender transgression. What I remembered were stories about looming poverty forestalled by a proper feminine performance—as if one could take *Pretty Woman* (minus the prostitution) as a serious how-to tale—and that hardly seemed likely to please this audience. The friends who chatted over dessert had never had to consider doing without the basics. They grew up upper-middle class, in families equipped to send them to college and ensure substantial support well into adulthood, or even throughout life if necessary. Refusing to conform had affected their choices and their sense of self, but life had given them no reason to think of conventional heterosexual femininity as a bulwark against homelessness. As for me, by the time I ventured to take my first community college classes, unprepared and unprovisioned, lacking support from parents or encouragement from teachers and counselors, I had conceived an embryonic wish: to climb over the verge and into a situation that would allow me to survive on my own.

Given my point of origin, the gender transgressions that mean so much to these women will always seem slightly off point to me, as do claims for the revolutionary promise of sex clubs or other unconventional sexual venues for women (of any origin or appetite). What they are all going for isn't revolution; what they want is just to be able to access their desires, to feel significant, and to be members of a community. They want the ordinary things that people want, and they happen to be living in a time and place where that is somewhat more possible for them than it is elsewhere. How could I become a member? How could I too belong? Finally I blurted, "All I remember is that I liked to have sex with girls."

Cheshire Calhoun (1998) argued that lesbians are displaced, and she contrasts that with the exclusion of heterosexual women from specific economic and social opportunities reserved primarily for men. Unlike exclusion, displacement "is a matter of having no legitimate place at all. The displaced are persons whom it would be functional for the system to eliminate—if not physically, at least by closeting their identity" (228). I would say, in contrast, that it is absolutely functional for "the system" to locate certain people—lesbians, the homeless, immigrants—at its outer limits. Who gets shoved up against the outer wall varies, but finding oneself there can be very uncomfortable. "System," furthermore, can refer on a smaller scale to lesbian communities, in which allying oneself with a suspect practice or belief—sadomasochism, radical feminism, butch, and femme—can mean instant almost-banishment.

More optimistic mappings are available, especially among those who exploit the connections between feminist and queer theory. For instance, Muñoz (1999) traced queer's lineage not only through Judith Butler, but also Monique Wittig and, especially, radical lesbians of color, including Cherríe Moraga, Gloria Anzaldúa, Audre Lorde, and Barbara Smith, focusing in particular on *This Bridge Called My Back* (1981). He noted that most scholars fail to engage with feminists of color seriously and critically; although some adore them from an awed distance. As a result, neither race nor feminism has been integrated into queer theory. Among those who trace the movement of sexuality across space and time, geographers stand out as particularly progressive, having used compelling queer-and- feminist mapping strategies, in one case to upset conventional homonormative origin stories, and in another to describe how "colliding epistemologies" informed the construction of a map of sites relating to gay and lesbian history.[6]

Invoking a metaphor of topographic features, Carolyn Dever (1997) used "dyke" to illustrate the functions of liminal identities in shaping feminist theory, and her metaphor applies as well to the broad patriarchal, heterosexually dominated system Calhoun spoke of. That system is comprised of all its parts; none are extraneous or unnecessary to it. However, the dyke cannot be recognized as a valid part of the system. If she were, the system could not remain what it is. The dyke must remain precisely where she is, so that everything else can remain stable. That may be quite uncomfortable, but it is not displacement.

Calhoun, drawing a distinction between male and heterosexual domination in order to situate lesbians as "family outlaws," argued that "the enactment of sexual desire, particularly for lesbians, is itself part of gender ambiguity. This is because desire for women is coded masculine; in addition, unlike the way it is for gay men, lesbian sexual excess is . . . an exit from the category 'woman'" (230). Unless I'm ready to dismiss other women's knowledge of their own lives, however, I must accept that for the others at the table, gender expression and sexual orientation really are securely bound together in a causal relation.

I can see the advantages of my friends' reality. They have a more self-assured sense of their identity as lesbians than I do. They have a sense of membership I lack. I have instead a queer story, a set of deconstructive strategies, a narrative of self that never lands on solid ground and lacks even the fleeting compensation of being avant-garde. In spite of the bits of autobiography I have included, the "I" of this story is only a perspective. "'I,'" as Virginia Woolf remarked, "is only a convenient term for somebody who has no real being" (4). The story begins like this: "I" assert active sexual desire, and that serves as an announcement of my departure from the category "woman."[7] I turn back to look at the identity I have exited—or been turned out of—and cannot be sure I was ever inside "woman" at all. And yet the forces of convention keep dragging my female body back toward her. I will never quite arrive and never fully leave. Who, if anyone, could fit snugly and securely inside her? The same thing happens with "lesbian," an identity category as unstable as "woman."

As it turns out (if anything can be said to come to completion in a story like this), the only thing I can be certain of is that the metaphoric dyke (or feminist, lesbian, or woman) the mainstream has been using to defend itself against the knowledge that it has nothing to defend itself against doesn't exist. Knowing that is no help at all, however, for those who are likely to be misidentified and suffer the consequences.

Change is hard

By comparison, defying one gender category in order to occupy another, even if the other category is understood as a hybrid, a female masculinity, seems too small a prize to be worth the price. Gender is not a medium that submits easily to the needs of someone who wants to shed the effects of social regulation in order to produce something new. Any performance of gender, no matter how parodic, cites the conventional forms. More importantly, the consequences of gender performances are too material to qualify as free play. Gender is elastic (it must be, or I never would have learned to perform femininity convincingly), but it partakes of dualities that although they can give pleasure can also produce a sense of confinement that is the antithesis of pleasure.

According to Annamarie Jagose (1996), "Queer, then, is an identity category that has no interest in consolidating or even stabilising itself. It maintains its critique of identity-focused movements by understanding that even the formation of its own coalitional and negotiated constituencies may well result in exclusionary and reifying effects far in excess of those intended." Leaving aside the question of which exclusions and reifications would not exceed queer intentions, Jagose went on to say that queer acknowledges "the inevitable violence of identity politics" and therefore has "no stake in its own hegemony." Allying itself with instability, queer theory nevertheless manages to preserve its own stable realm where it "maintains its critique of identity-focused movements." Although Jagose recognized that queer theory might be used to establish exclusive identity categories, her phrasing veiled the question of agency, making it difficult to ask who in particular might want to use queer theory to establish hegemony. In the absence of a subject, queer theory appears to act as its own agent, attempting to establish homeostasis as it acts on and stands up against forces with no bodies. Passive constructions ("may well result . . . even the formation of . . . ") allowed Jagose to avoid naming who represents the threat and who will act to preserve queer theory's mission.

We can't know precisely who they are, but those who accept the deconstruction of their identities and remain true to the spirit of Queer are the changed, the enlightened, prisoners freed from the pre-Platonic cave. Everyone else is consigned to a world of rigid but baseless categories, where they function as reified objects of deconstructive critique, the necessary Others whose names allow queer to know its own difference.

But none of this is real. Queer theory lacks agency, so it cannot yield up any means of distinguishing between freedom and confinement. Assuming that queers renounce the categories that distinguish inside from outside, they (we?) cannot exclude nonqueers from their (our?) theoretical region, because that region is borderless, unstable, and constantly under revision.

Jagose claimed that Queer has no interest in consolidating itself, but the tendency in much queer thought to dissociate sexual practice from gender expression and queer thought from feminism tends to consolidate the field around those distinctions. In response to the pressure to establish some secure position from which to speak, the queer thinker cannot claim to know what a woman is, but she can claim that gender, as feminist theory has analyzed it, is binary, reified, and heterosexist, and that therefore feminists lack the means of seeing sex as other than oppressive to women.

Old school

Although it is true that feminists managed to lay the groundwork to make feminism a marginally authoritative discourse by institutionalizing feminist thought in women's studies, it has never managed to entrench itself as the more traditional academic disciplines have done. Biddy Martin (2001) contradicted this, saying that women's studies is now institutionalized "on equal footing with other academic and administrative units" (353). Having succeeded in identifying useful critical practices and defining a proper object (that object, though unnamed at this point in Martin's text, is probably "women"), women's studies "lost much of its critical and intellectual vigor" (353). The object herself apparently did us in. Women's studies was "plagued from the outset by the exclusions its self-definition entails" (354).

Perhaps because I have never worked in a large and well-supported women's studies program, my first response is simply to observe that very few programs have achieved parity with other academic units. Programs remain only because they typically more than pay for themselves in terms of numbers of students served and (dare I say it?) academic quality. I fail to recognize as typical the self-righteous, cynical academic feminism Martin described. Martin recommended developing "a certain fearlessness about the differences within feminist studies, even those that appear to threaten its identity as a field or a political project" (379). Few feminists approach their differences without fear or defensiveness, but that is largely because "woman" is a trickster who mortifies anyone who tries to anchor her to a final position. The women's studies programs I have worked with have evolved rapidly; they have survived intellectually and materially because feminists learned not to entrench themselves in a canon or hide behind "woman."

Martin imagined a future for women's or gender studies, for feminism, and for queer studies because she saw evidence that misogyny and homophobia persist. Announcements of the death of feminism, however, proliferate. Hypotheses about the cause of death vary: Young women don't identify as victims, so feminism is dead. Feminism has become part of the establishment, so feminism is dead. American secular/white/heterosexual/lesbian feminism can't stand up to the challenges of Islamic or woman-of-color or sex-positive feminism, so feminism is dead. The American turn toward the Right, the war in Iraq, terrorism, and television have all killed feminism. A few extremely privileged ivy league women decided not to climb the corporate ladder. Therefore, feminism is dead.

In the mid-1990s, I submitted an essay critiquing the discourse of rights in liberal feminism for inclusion in a book the editors had given the unwieldy title *Teaching, Thinking, Writing Social Justice.* When it was ultimately published in 2000, the book's title had suffered a transformation; it was now *Is Academic Feminism Dead?* According to the introduction, the editors were responding to what they read in the newspapers: "Feminists are charged with the death of the family as a site of social stability, and with the death of the university as a site of objective knowledge production. At the same time, we are alleged to have succumbed to irrelevance: feminism is proclaimed dead with almost comical regularity" (3).

The editors decided, much to my relief, that feminism was still alive after all. They were concerned that antifeminists could appropriate our critiques of feminism and use them against us. However, the editors felt that publishing the essays was useful not only because feminists benefit from self-critique, but because we—the authors—collectively disproved the antifeminist accusation that feminism is a monolith.

I was surprised to find that I was among those drafted to defend feminism from its death notices, because I don't take such apocalyptic announcements seriously. The title *Is Academic Feminism Dead?* is a sellout. It is catchier than *Teaching Social Justice,* but it panders to the interests of those who so regularly announce the death of feminism. It allows antifeminists to set the terms of our discourse.

However, I appreciate the efforts of those who take the time to challenge the inaccuracies and misrepresentations of attacks like those mounted in the 1990s by Christina Hoff Sommers and Daphne Patai. One such writer, Carol Sternhell (1994), summed up the difference between her own knowledge of women's studies programs and Sommers's portrayal of feminism as the illegitimate usurper of institutional authority:

> As someone who has spent most of the last 25 years on one college campus or another, I'm stunned by Sommers' portrayal of university life. Where I see small, underfunded women's studies programs, she sees monoliths of thought control; where I see attempts to make traditional curricula less exclusionary, she sees the vicious destruction of Western culture; where I see faculties that are still predominantly white and predominantly male, she sees a vast network of feminist deans and search committees who refuse to hire anyone who doesn't toe the party line. (2)

When I encounter conservative attacks on women's studies, I receive in a flash the same vision of power I had when I read the end-of-the-world fantasies that sprang into being at the crossroads where psychology and medicine met right-wing religion: What if there really were a good old girls' network of feminist and lesbian administrators? What if we could end the world as we know it and claim all the postapocalyptic space for our own millennial dream? What if "we" had a party line and could make people toe it?

According to Daphne Patai (1998), "we" do. She wrote, "feminist intolerance and self-righteousness contributed to a situation in which heterosexual women are made to feel that they are not 'real' feminists. Aware of being 'compromised' by their attachments to men, such women have often acted apologetic toward their lesbian feminist colleagues and friends" (10). Perhaps bending under the weight of feminist intolerance, Patai did not say that lesbians make heterosexual women feel bad. Instead, lesbians are the passive objects of the apologetic actions of heterosexual women. But the net effect of all the apologizing heterosexual women do is that they do not feel very welcome in academic feminism. They are victims of "heterophobia," which has made them outsiders, romantically attached to men but unable to dignify that attachment in women's studies, where men and heterosexual love have been tagged as the enemies of women's liberation. In *Heterophobia,* women's studies is rather neatly organized around its antiheterosexual imperialism. The colonizers—those who have forced good heterosexual women to accept their guilt, assume victim status, or leave the field—must be lesbians, since they are the only ones who might benefit from the otherwise destructive effects of heterophobia. However, no one could accuse Patai of actually saying that the lesbian agenda has taken over or that lesbians have done anything to incite heterosexual shame.

Wendy Brown (1997), in contrast to right-wing critics, saw women's studies as lacking a party line. Instead, in her view, women's studies is lost and panicked amid contradictory questions about its worth and direction. In the absence of anything real to organize around, it is merely obsessed with preserving itself within the structures of academia. She listed among the phenomena that "ravaged" women's studies in the 1980s "wars" over theory, race, and sex, followed by the advent of Critical Race Theory, post-colonial and queer theory, and cultural studies (83). According to Brown, women's studies professors responded by seeking to "preserve the realm" and have "resisted, restricted, or worse, colonized" these theoretical endeavors and fields of study. "Each, therefore, is compelled to go elsewhere, while women's studies consolidates itself in the remains, impoverished by the lack of challenges from within, bewildered by its new ghettoization in the academy—this time by feminists themselves" (83–84).

I see things differently. I recall feminists actively generating the "race, sex and theory" debates that so rapidly expanded the terrain of what was thinkable as women's studies. Brown would perhaps condemn as imperialist my assertion that women's studies is a suitable place to do theory and studies of culture, sexuality, and race. If so, she would agree with my students in queer theory, who dismissed as imperialist *Amazon to Zami*, the book I cited earlier in which A. R. and Rais Nur's essay on Malaysian lesbians appeared. I introduced it in the classroom with high expectations, hoping for an energetic discussion about the specific cultural and political differences the wide array of authors revealed. My students, however, believed that the editor of the volume, Monika Reinfelder, a German women's studies scholar, had "colonized" disadvantaged women of color around the world by soliciting their essays for *Amazon to Zami* and by using "feminism" and "lesbian" in the book's subtitle, tactics oppressors use to "name the other." The fact that all the contributors were identified as lesbian and were invested in feminism and women's movements did nothing to allay my students' skepticism. It would have been different if the Malaysian, Indonesian, Filipina, South African, Namibian, Costa Rican, Chilean, Zimbabwean, and Argentinean contributors had been the editors of the book; if they had been in charge, the book might speak something like the truth.

Because of her professional, geographical, economic, and racial positioning, Reinfelder was better able to do the work of editing and publishing the volume than most, if not all, of the contributors. The dangerous political environment that caused Nur and A. R. to write under pseudonyms could well be enough to prevent their carrying out a similar project. Contributing to the kinds of positive changes that would enable lesbians across the globe to speak freely and to live comfortably is the goal of each of the contributors as well as the editor. If we agree to the thinking that Brown and my students proposed, however, all the Reinfelders, the privileged white teachers and scholars of women's studies from the United States or Europe, would have to resign, or less dramatically, would not include among the texts they publish or assign to students anything by women unlike themselves. To do so would be imperialistic. Not to do so, however, would be xenophobic and racist. The way out of this "damned if you do, damned if you don't" stalemate is to keep pressing for the rights of those who, for whatever reasons, can't name themselves publicly, which is what Reinfelder and many others are trying, in ways both effective and bumbling, to do.

In fact, the phenomena Brown posited as Other to women's studies overlap it, offering evidence of its interdisciplinary character and tendency to transform over time. But as my failed attempt to interest students in *Amazon to Zami* suggests, taking up feminism as an institutional practice offers one daily opportunities to learn humility and the limits of one's power to effect change. Feminism suffers twice by its dogged interest in women: once at a theoretical level because the term "woman" represents a highly suspicious identity category even within feminist thought, and (again, ironically) because most women are easy to identify as such in the everyday world. If, in common with Patai and Hoff Sommers, one wants to find fault with women (or feminists, or lesbians) who teach women's studies, their actions are readily available for review and critique.

Women and teachers of women's studies are as variable in their ethics and common sense as everyone else is. They are as likely as others to make false accusations and generate unproductive conflicts. Motivated by bias or personal ambition, women's studies scholars try to exclude those whose ways of thinking or sheer presence seem like a threat. The difference of women's studies isn't that it is more free of human frailty than any other human endeavor. Its difference is political. Women's studies deliberately presents itself as place not just for scholarship, but for advocating the rights of women, and in doing so, opens itself to all sorts of attacks. There come, from one direction, ad hominem attacks and generalizations, based on the kind of juicy anecdotes that make Patai's and Hoff Sommers's work (among others) so appealing to the right wing.[8] From other directions come announcements of imminent or already accomplished catastrophe by disillusioned feminists, queer theorists, unsympathetic administrators, and anyone who was ever done wrong by a woman.[9]

Future practical

How can queer theory avoid a similar fate? It is more glamorous than women's studies, but fashions change. Setting up any academic operation poses risks, and even theorists who have no other object than to deconstruct sexual identities have to set up their equipment somewhere. However, if queer studies can seem to function in a relatively abstract realm, dissociated from the material lives of its constituencies, it could elude the worst of the attacks that women's studies now spends most of its efforts fending off. Then queer could embed itself in mainstream academia far more effectively than feminism has. Michael Warner argued that queer "represents, among other things, an aggressive impulse of generalization; it rejects a minoritizing logic of toleration or simple political interest—representation in favor of a more thorough resistance to regimes of the normal" (1993, xxvi). Distancing oneself from the political interests of a specific group and claiming instead to represent "an impulse" means avoiding messy conflicts about who really fits within the parameters of the generalizer's model. Queer studies might, by claiming to address the interests of anyone who at any point perceives herself or himself or others as deviant from the normal, operate like traditional social liberalism and thus avoid being stigmatized as feminism has. That may be the sacrifice that makes survival possible.

If in addition queer studies can be read as postfeminist in the apocalyptic sense, it might succeed, paradoxically, as a less troubling alternative to women's studies. Sternhell's summary of the myths right-wing opportunists propagate about women's studies is not very different from the list of criticisms queer can make about feminism: that feminism represents a regulatory regime; that it seeks to destroy the freedom to express divergent versions of gender and sexuality; that its "members" are over privileged and out of touch with prevailing cultural and social ideals. Queer also shares with the right wing the underlying conviction that feminism should die.

However, even if queer theorists succeed in representing not a group of people but the impulse to generalize, they still need to feel that there is something like ground under their feet. Women's studies founded itself on the conviction that women are real and that it is possible to construct a world of knowledge about them, and that conviction led to a series of border wars—not an unusual consequence of establishing a new academic field. The pressure to establish a defensible position, whether on the strength of one's own projection of mastery, on the supposedly dead body of an opponent, or on the basis of solid, useful, and provable ideas, is everywhere in academia. Neither women's studies nor queer studies has escaped that pressure.

Of the existing dangers, the most important is that uninitiated students and faculty don't grasp the nuances of queer theory's critiques any more than they understand the turns of feminist theory. Many of them will join the general public in imagining that queer simply means homosexual, and that queer studies advocates for people who occupy a discreet identity category and whose behavior, morality, worthiness, and rights to the classroom are open to question. Women's studies and queer studies have this much in common: neither has the power to stifle uninformed judgments that say their work is the fabrication of a "special interest group" no bigger than the committee of self-obsessed cultural elites who approved the course of study.

Wendy Brown's belief that women's studies tries to "colonize" other theoretical discourses in order to preserve a shrinking "realm" suggests how tempting it is to imagine that theory belongs to actual people, either an indigenous population with rights to that theoretical space or a group of cultural and intellectual parasites. If I apply the colonization metaphor to queer theory, as Brown does, feminism only has rights to Judith Butler's feminist ideas. A feminist who uses Judith Butler's queer ideas, whichever those might be, trespasses on the real estate marked off by and for queer people. She (the feminist who agrees not to colonize other theoretical discourses) might be stumped by the question of how to differentiate one Butlerian idea from another, but at least she knows she must drop Foucault altogether.

If I seem to press this point to a ridiculous degree, it is because it is only possible to appreciate how ridiculous the "colonization" metaphor is by spelling it out. Each of the theoretical discourses and fields women's studies is supposed to have colonized only achieve integrity to the degree that they too draw from multiple disciplines and racial, sexual, and gendered perspectives. Women's studies, the reviled colonizer, could be excluded from the network of exchange, but only if all the interdisciplinary fields ceased to exist and the people in them went away to do other things.

As with women's studies, so with "woman." Rejecting feminine imperialism was the basis of the "Is Trans the New Butch?" panel and of Inness's and Lloyd's wish to establish the butch as a rebel loner in "Barbieland." Robin Maltz's definition of "stone butch" as an identity that "lives with the contradiction of masculinity inscribed on a female body" was more promising in its acknowledgment of the interdependence of sex/gender categories (1998, 275). To be worthy of the name, however, her stone butch must not identify as a woman. The stone butch must be clear of traces of femininity, which for Maltz has no "realness," but is instead comprised of sexual objectification and receptivity. Femininity can play either the rapacious colonizer or the helplessly colonized.

All in all, I have more respect for the version of femininity I was taught as a girl. That femininity held at its core not the romance, beauty, and playfulness it projected, but unapologetically economic goals. What counted as "real" for my mother and grandmother wasn't the perfection of the performance, as important as that was. What was real was the living the performance was designed to earn. Conventional femininity is rough way to make a living, even if you're very good at it, but it is as honest as the working day is long.

About vowels

What about women—or "womyn"—who are indifferent to the demands of conventional femininity and yet claim to have a separate female identity at least as real as that of butch or trans? What happens when they claim to have established a homeland in geographical space and refuse to be receptive to masculine incursions?

According to a report in the lesbian news magazine *Off Our Backs*, "Eight transgender activists . . . were asked to leave the Michigan Womyn's Music Festival this year [2000]. The eight were escorted to the Main Gate of the festival, their attendance wristbands were cut off, and they were expelled from the grounds. In keeping with Festival policy, their entrance fees were not refunded" (Mantilla, 8).

The organizers of the yearly Michigan Festival permitted only "womyn born womyn" to attend. The term includes those who are genetically female, were raised as females, and have always identified as female. Vowels were substituted in order to render femaleness independent of the masculine referent embedded in the term "women." The policy promised not to question the gender identity of those who wished to be admitted, but anyone who denied being a womon-born womon was asked to leave. The transgendered activists had done just that in order to protest the policy. A Camp Trans press release quoted one transgendered activist: "We don't identify as 'womyn-born womyn'—we don't know what it even means or why it should be used against us or our trannie friends."

Like the term "woman-identified woman," which some preferred over "lesbian," "womon-born womon" names itself twice, its two subjects reinforcing each other's existence. The womon-born womon identity is an affront to queer sensibilities in part because it redefines "lesbian" as a matter of reproductive solidarity rather than sexual desire. But there is nothing new in the intolerance queer thought generates for womyn-born womyn. Within the sex/gender structures queer seeks to deconstruct, "woman" has always lacked integrity, existing not of her own accord but as masculinity's abject but receptive other. "Woman" is always already deconstructed, so when queer points out that the boundaries of her body or her land are (or should be) penetrable by those who identify as masculine, it only replicates conventional thinking.

Womon-born womon is as real an identity as stone butch or trans. All attempt to create and defend a conceptual territory, an imaginary ground for beleaguered sex/gender identities. What makes the Michigan Womyn's Music Festival different is that its founders thought that "womyn" should have land, a specific geographical location for creating a community around the identity. That stroke of separatist boldness offends both conventional and queer thinking about what "woman" means. Over the almost three decades of their existence, the land and its womyn have produced enough fiery criticism from feminists, nonfeminist men, lesbians, and now transgendered activists to burn the festival to the ground.

Lisa Vogel, producer of the Michigan Womyn's Music Festival, said in a 2000 statement about the transgender conflict, "it saddens me that the young womyn we used to call 'baby-dykes' are now growing up questioning the validity of the very concept of being female" (Koyama, 51). When she defined the transgendered activists as "womyn," Vogel applied to the transgendered activists identity categories they don't apply to themselves, refused to grant "trans" the respect she grants to her own identity, "womon-born womon." Similarly, Sheila Jeffreys refused to apply to transgendered people the gendered pronouns they apply to themselves. Alix Dobkin (2000), joining Vogel in mourning the lost "baby dykes," demonstrated how the politics of identity determine who counts among the lost: "To my eyes and ears, young butch dykes walking the FTM (female-to-male) path look and despite vocal alteration, sound, quite like the young butch Dykes many of us have been and known for decades. However, these days we hear mostly their echoes and see only their backs as they flee womanhood.

But they are our line, and by rejecting their female bodies along with our shared history, they break our hearts." Dobkin, mixing what might be a genuine sense of loss with a patronizing assumption that she knows FTMs better than they know themselves, urged them to reclaim femaleness and rejoin dyke history.

All players in the drama—the queers and the lesbian feminists—were vying for the authority to name the "Other." The womyn-born womyn were defending against what they saw as the attempted obliteration of their identity and the invasion by outsiders of the scrap of land that affirms that identity. The transgendered activists' refusal to recognize "womyn-born womyn" as real meant that they could not see the women who founded and ran the festival as another group of marginalized people attempting to build and maintain community. The challenges from transactivists appear to many lesbian feminists as one more phase in a long history of hostile efforts to deny their existence.

"Womon" is as easily deconstructible as "woman" or "transgender" or any other sex/gender identity, but deconstructing someone else's identity against their will is a vicious act, unless that identity represents a high degree of privilege.[10] This is true when, like Jeffreys, one portrays the other identity as groundless while reserving authenticity for one's own. It is still true when queer theorists or activists refuse to respect the self-naming of womyn-born womyn who decline to cooperate with the deconstruction of their identity.

It is possible to find more respectful strategies close at hand. The Michigan Womyn's Music Festival's official statement on the transgender controversy insisted on the viability of "womon-born womon," but did so without exhibiting the disrespect for transgendered people's power to name themselves evident in Vogel's personal statements: "Claiming one week a year as womyn-born womyn space is not in contradiction to being trans-positive and trans-allies. . . . We believe there is room for all affinity groups to enjoy separate and supportive space, and also to come together in broader alliances to fight prejudice that affects all of us" (Koyama, 39). A number of MTFs supported this official statement. One transgendered woman declared that although she could pass as a "womon-born womon," she chose not to attend the Michigan festival because she believed that "a line must be drawn somewhere and I would rather be on the wrong side of such a line than for none to be drawn at all."[11] Another transgendered woman, addressing a nontransgendered man who thought it outrageous that the Michigan festival admits only women, suggested why even those who can argue convincingly that they belong at an all-woman festival believe that the festival would lose its reason for being if everyone were allowed to attend: "I look forward to a day when all women, trans and non, are able to spend time together on the land simply as women without men being present. . . . Should you somehow manage to force inclusion of men, you will destroy the event." Another woman who agreed with the need to establish separate space hopes "to offer a feeling that genetic women can feel safe with me in their presence."

These are the women—those who feel the need to build alliances and those who understand why "drawing a line" is important—who stand the best chance of re-creating the space of the Michigan Festival so that it includes MTFs. Their allusion to the need of "affinity" groups to have access to separate space hearkens back to the "Combahee River Collective Statement," a classic women's studies text dating from 1977, which described the difficult process through which the Boston black feminist collective created enough space and time alone together to formulate an agenda for their own liberation. They decided to focus on their own oppression as the best contribution they could make to the liberation of all oppressed people, and they cited identity as the conceptual basis for their decision: "We believe that the most profound and potentially most radical politics come directly out of our own identity, as opposed to working to end somebody else's oppression. In the case of Black women this is a particularly repugnant, dangerous, threatening, and therefore revolutionary concept because it is obvious from looking at all the political movements that have preceded us that anyone is more worthy of liberation than ourselves" (212).

Unlike the women of the Combahee collective, the womyn-born womyn of the Michigan festival will not be seen to exist in racial terms. Whiteness dominates their group but doesn't comprise the whole, and that will go unremarked except by those who have reason to pay particular attention to race. This kind of erasure brings with it economic and social advantages that do not accrue to people who are marked racially. From the perspective of most people who do not identify as womyn-born womyn, however, their gender identity is nonexistent in another way: they are read as inauthentic and unworthy of recognition.

Impure Thoughts

All of these modes of separation turn on one another, appearing successively or simultaneously as oppression, privilege, and resistance. These are not pure states, and determining the real case requires asking questions about whose agency is at work at any given turn. Evelyn Hammonds's contribution to *Feminism Meets Queer Theory* (1997) insisted on the specificity of black women's sexuality in terms that emphasized the difficulty of black women's being seen to exist as proper agents of their own sexual desire: "Black women's sexuality is often described in metaphors of speechlessness, space, or vision, as a 'void' or empty space that is simultaneously ever visible (exposed) and invisible and where black women's bodies are always already colonized." The sexuality of black women is seen to exist only in relation to the white (but racially unmarked) colonizer, so what is seen is not what really is. "What is"—the reality of black women's sexuality—exists in a separate, private space. This separate space is not chosen freely. Those who occupy it lack the social privileges that permit white people to enjoy either privacy or visibility and to exercise choice about how their sexuality will be defined and when their sexuality will be publicly visible.

One problem with the distinction Hammonds drew between black women's and white women's sexuality is that the latter appeared to her to be readable and clear. Hammonds situated "white woman" very much as "lesbian" or "feminist" or "women's studies" is situated in relation to queer. She recommended that we not assume "that black female sexualities are structured along an axis of normal and perverse paralleling that of white women" because this assumption is part of what prevents us from seeing the reality of black women's sexuality (150). Black women's desires could exist "in dynamic relationship rather than in opposition"; they might well desire both "women and men simultaneously" (150). To produce a vision of black women's sexuality as dynamic and multiple, Hammonds relied on the supposedly stable arrangement of white women's sexuality according to conventional oppositions (lesbian/heterosexual) and clinical values (normal/perverse). If black women's sexuality is an unexplored space, white women's sexuality must have been fully mapped.

Trying to discern the meaning of the silences of others is a perilous business. In the introduction, I discussed my own anxious attempt to produce a conventional vision of love. My sexual life since that early point can be interpreted in any number of ways. The evidence can certainly be coerced into fitting the conventions Hammonds assigned to white women and traditional psychology assigns to racially unmarked lesbians. However, the shape of my sexuality doesn't fit any more comfortably into that interpretation than black women's sexuality fits the configurations white racism and heterosexism have assigned to them.

For this reason, when Hammonds quoted Darlene Clark Hine, who described how black women "created the appearance of openness and disclosure but actually shielded the truth of their inner lives and selves from their oppressors," I experienced a jolt of recognition (143). This happened just before a disapproving inner voice told me that if I discovered any sort of commonality across racial lines, that would make me a white colonizer invading the separate space of black female sexuality. And yet the pattern Hine describes is familiar: the construction of a facade of openness, the knowledge that behind that facade there is a self that knows different, and the certainty that survival depends on hiding that truth.

This is a solitary exercise because I have no viable identity around which to form a community. I can't ascribe my experience to oppression by race, certainly, but neither can I find myself in the queer deconstructions of "lesbian," gender or sexuality. I can imagine the sense of security and belonging the womyn-born womyn are seeking to create, but "womon-born womon" fits no better. After all these years, therefore, the queer girl's protective strategies still appeal. I offer up a publicly conventional picture in daily life so that I can retire occasionally and search for some breathing space, some privacy, in the here and now. This space is hedged about by the material politics of sex and gender, race and class, as green space in the city is surrounded by concrete and noise. I prize it all the more for its risky location. The panic I felt as a fifth grader, when I feared the substitute teacher would discover my kind of love—my breathing space—and try to take it away, was also the moment when I began to be conscious that I had something valuable to lose. I am therefore permanently uneasy about accepting the authority of anyone or anything that acts systematically to regulate thought and behavior, that assesses worth by categorical fit, canonical approval, or popular endorsement.

Notes

Chapter 1. Rats and Women

1. Studies of women with CAH (Congenital Adrenal Hyperplasia) have not come to firm conclusions about its influence on sexual orientation or gender performance. It would also be difficult to determine to what degree the influence of CAH, the timing of the diagnosis, or the various treatments and genital surgeries that can follow a diagnosis most affect a woman's sexual life. A. A. Ehrhardt, D. Evers, and J. Money (1968) found some homosexual fantasies and experiences in women with CAH. Twenty years later, Money and Lewis reported on two children with congenital adrenal hyperplasia who were studied until they were adults. The authors infer that both were prenatally "ultramasculinized," which prevented postnatal influences on sexual orientation from affecting them. A. Lev-Ran (1974) found no incidences of homosexual experience or fantasy among women with CAH. Bidlingmaier et al. (1982) reported, "The majority of the patients was [*sic*] not handicapped in heterosexual life." R. W. Dittmann et al. (1992) found increased homosexual experiences among CAH women in comparison with their non-CAH sisters. Since the mid-1990s, studies of the gender identities and sexualities of intersexed people have burgeoned, and attempts to ascribe lesbianism in non-intersexed women to the influence of hormones have retreated without altogether disappearing.

2. See, for example, G. Dörner and G. Hinz (1972), G. Dörner and J. Fatschel (1970), and G. Dörner et al. (1968).

3. For instance, W. Perloff (1949) concluded that "homosexuality is a purely psychologic phenomenon, neither dependent on a hormonal pattern for its production nor amenable by endocrine substances to change" (139).

4. See, for instance, J. Loehlin and D. McFadden (2003), D. McFadden (2003), Q. Rahman (2005), R. A. Lippa (2003), and W. M. Brown (2002); regarding the effects of pregnant women smoking, see L. Ellis and S. Cole-Harding (2001).

5. Roy Baumeister (2004) promotes this view, remarking that "female sexuality is inherently more amenable than male sexuality to influence by cultural events, historical circumstances, socialization, peer influence, and other social variables" (133). He considers it indisputable that women don't experience a level of sexual desire equal to men's and sees that difference as the origin of women's sexual plasticity. Baumeister, Roy F. 2004. "Gender and Erotic Plasticity: Sociocultural Influences on the Sex Drive." *Sexual and Relationship Therapy 19 (2)*: 133–39.

6. In an anthropological study of scientists in the laboratory, Bruno Latour and Steve Woolgar (1986) addressed their various ideological perspectives, noting, "Even in the small group [of scientists] studied here, the representations of the world, or ideologies, differ markedly . . . . One had a typically positivistic representation of science borrowed from Claude Bernard (1865); another had a mystical view of science and linked his work to a fundamentalist approach to religion; a third had a business-like view of his activity and held to the epistemology of a nouveau riche; a fourth worked with an economical model of investments" (230n2). It would be difficult to argue credibly that such differential views, brought to bear on an object of study as contentious as homosexuality, would fail to influence at a minimum the construction of research questions and interpretations of data.

7. John Money (1987) cited experiments with various animals demonstrating that depending on when testosterone is administered to the female fetus it is possible to "masculinize" her brain structure, producing more mounting and socially aggressive behaviors in the resulting adult female, but without affecting external genitalia (388–89). It is also possible to alter genitals but not brain structure, or to alter both. Money described the experimental animals as "more or less . . . hormonal robots insofar as a masculine or a feminine mating pattern can be foreordained on the basis of regulating the prenatal hormonalization of the brain" (389), whereas humans are more influenced by environment via sensory inputs, which Money takes to be part of a system that is wholly biological. Any theory that fails to understand that biology is everything is, in Money's view, "spookological" (393).

8. Havelock Ellis (1897) maintained that although "the chief characteristic of the sexually inverted woman is a certain degree of masculinity," some heterosexual women also had a predilection for men's clothes and masculine manners (94).

9. There is no agreement on what a lesbian body build is. In the same year that Dörner's rat study appeared, F. E. Kenyon (1968a) examined 123 lesbians and found that they tend to be shorter and heavier than "controls" (presumed heterosexual women). Although heterosexual women had more symptoms of premenstrual "tension," lesbians tended to resent menstruation more, an indication of their reluctance to accept female gender roles. In another article published the same year, Kenyon questioned lesbians on whether they had been raised as if they were boys, enjoyed dressing in masculine clothes, or had been seduced into homosexuality, all questions that would have applied to the invert of yesteryear, and implying that gender performance and sexual dominance and submission are important in defining a lesbian identity (1968b). Muriel Perkins (1981) cited anthropometric data indicating "that the homosexual women have narrower hips, increased arm and leg girths, less subcutaneous fat, and more muscle than heterosexual women" (337). More recently, Anthony Bogaert (1998) reviewed the data on women gathered by the Kinsey Institute, and found that lesbians considered themselves to be taller and heavier than heterosexual women; Bogaert suggested that lesbians are more likely to align with masculine characteristics.

10. Attempts to confirm hormonal influences on lesbians' social and sexual roles persist. S. M. Pearcey et al. (1996), in a study that tested levels of testosterone in "butch" and "femme" lesbians works from a premise akin to Dörner's, proposed that gendered "sex role" behaviors might correlate with hormone levels. Unfortunately, they did not raise the question of how the gendered behaviors they used to differentiate butches from

femmes might affect testosterone levels. Analyzing heterosexuality and transsexuality, Eli Coleman et al. (1989) concluded that there was no evidence that hormones influence sexual identities or behaviors. C. P. Dancey (1990) found no evidence to support a proposition that hormonal influences might leave traces that would distinguish "primary" lesbians (who had never had sexual contact with men) from "secondary" lesbians (who had prior sexual contact with men). His set of categories corresponded roughly to Dörner's predominantly and completely homosexual rats. John Bancroft (1994) believed that sexual orientation probably does have a genetic component, but that psychological and social factors are most important. Although N. Gartrell et al. (1977) found that testosterone levels of lesbians were substantially higher than those of heterosexual women, A. Banks and N. Gartrell (1995) concluded that there was no good evidence that hormones determine sexual orientation. However, as late as 1999, the argument that androgens cause homosexuality still had some currency, represented in another article by D. Singh proposing that the difference between butch lesbians and femme lesbians might be "caused by differential exposure to prenatal androgens" (1035). W. James (2005) picked up on the same proposition in an article about biosocial influences on sexual orientation.

Chapter 2. Being Perverse

1. According to some studies, approximately one of five college men reported having sex with a woman without her consent (Koss and Oros 1982; Peterson and Franzese 1987). Garrett-Gooding and Senter (1987) found that between 25 percent and 50 percent of college men reported being sexually aggressive. Other studies (Rapaport and Burkhart 1984; Greendlinger and Byrne 1987; and Tieger 1981) showed that about 35 percent of college men admitted they might rape or coerce a woman sexually. In spite of the growing awareness of sexual assault, studies in the early 1990s did not show much progress. A study performed in 1992 and reported in 1996 found about the same percentages of men would commit sexual assault as earlier studies found (Osland et al. 1996). According to Malamuth et al. (1991), one of thirteen college men admitted anonymously that they had sexually assaulted a woman, and approximately 50 percent of college males admitted they would sexually assault a woman if they knew that they would not be found out.

2. Chris Wilson, a former police officer, was sentenced to five years probation for maintaining a Web site that gave free access to pornography to military personnel in exchange for pictures of Iraqi war dead. It was the pornography, not the posting of violent images, that led to his conviction. "Probation over website," *New York Times*, April 23, 2006. http://www.nytimes.com/2006/04/23/us/23bodies.html.

3. Bureau of Justice Statistics Crime Data Brief, Intimate Partner Violence, 1993–2001, February 2003.

4. Comment by Anthony Jordan, head of the committee that drafted the amendment. The relevant portion of the amendment reads: "The husband and wife are of equal worth before God, since both are created in God's image. The marriage relationship models the way God relates to his people. A husband is to love his wife as Christ loved the church. He has the God-given responsibility to provide for, to protect, and to lead his family. A wife is to submit herself graciously to the servant leadership of her husband even as the church willingly submits to the headship of Christ. She, being in the image

of God, as is her husband, and thus equal to him, has the God-given responsibility to respect her husband and to serve as his helper in managing the household and nurturing the next generation" ("Love, Honor & Obey?," *The News Hour with Jim Lehrer* (transcript), June 10, 1998).

5. And it seems that women are wise to refuse subordinate status in marriage. Women who are unhappily married are more vulnerable than their unhappy husbands to various health problems; most dramatically, wives who have less decision-making power than their husbands are at a higher risk of death (Coontz, 310). Where women could obtain a divorce unilaterally, the rate of suicide among married women dropped by 20 percent and the rate of domestic violence also dropped (Coontz, 293).

6. Coontz cites John Locke, Mary Wollstonecraft, the Marquise de Condorcet, and Mary Astell as early proponents of equality for women and more egalitarian marriages (148–49).

7. As Norman O. Brown (1966) put it, "Freud seems to project into prehistoric times the constitutional crisis of seventeenth-century England" (3). Pateman, however, went further: "Freud's stories make explicit that power over women and not only freedom is at issue before the original agreement is made, and he also makes clear that two realms are created through the original pact" (1988, 12). Those two regions are the public and domestic spheres.

8. Most of the liberals I know would deny both of these claims, but they feel best about lesbians and gays whose identities and relationship patterns can be thought of as virtually heterosexual (only the sex of the partner differs), and they grow uncomfortable around anyone who challenges these notions. Then there are the well-meaning parents who tell their gay children that homosexuality may be a phase, implying they might still be able to pursue the biological and psychological imperative of heterosexuality when they are more mature.

9. This might explain why Hobbes, "more than most, was concerned with the preservation of order at all costs. Indeed, through his political solution, he sacrificed all public debate and discussion; he sacrificed all populist implications of his consent theory and opted instead for absolutism; and finally he sacrificed politics itself to public order in the state" (Wright 2002, 133).

10. See, for instance, J. Jureidini (2001), R. Stoller (1975), and J. Chasseguet-Smirgel (1991).

11. Rousseau also referred to greater and smaller families and spoke directly to the differences between the state and the patriarchal family. The necessity of a male-headed hierarchy, however, is consistent between them (4–5). Jeremy Bentham (1891) discovered what he considered the difference between society and the family in the idea of continuity. Children are subject to their parents only while they are dependent on them, so the family is more ephemeral than political society. This would be a good point except that some version of "the family" reproduces itself in every generation; it matters less which people are at the head of any particular family than that the family have a head (140).

12. Referring to "religion, morality, and social sense," Freud (1927) wrote, "It seems that the male sex has taken the lead in developing all of these moral acquisitions; and that they have then been transmitted to women by cross-inheritance" (49–50).

13. Hobbes had more hope for men's basic nature than Freud had. "And thus much for the ill condition, which man by meer Nature is actually placed in; though with a pos-

sibility to come out of it, consisting partly in the Passions, partly in his Reason" (85–86). In Hobbes's vision, even when men are miserable in a state of nature, where there are no civilized people and no laws to prevent murder or incest, men always have the chance of (re)gaining order through the application of reason and passion. Together, these basic human attributes direct man to improve his lot by agreeing to be subject to a common power that will protect his rights.

14. According to Freud, "the masses are lazy and unintelligent; they have no love for instinctual renunciation, and they are not to be convinced by argument of its inevitability; and the individuals composing them support one another in giving free reign to their indiscipline. It is only through the influence of individuals who can set an example and whom masses recognize as their leaders that they can be induced to perform the work and undergo the renunciations on which the existence of civilization depends" (1964, 7–8).

15. Trusting that one's authority resides in one's knowledge of a sovereign agent is part of the masquerade of the modest witness (Haraway 1997) I referred to in the introduction. Her modest witness could uncover the secrets of nature (or, in the case of perversion, secret violations of natural law) without having to reveal the secret of his own position. The authoritative healer, by contrast, has to reveal something of himself in order to get close enough to the disordered body or spirit to effect a healing. Pointing up to an extrinsic power allows him to draw attention away from the fallibility of his revealed self.

16. That gesture has become commonplace, although psychoanalysts often read others' denial as confirmation of their theories, just as they can see a patient's resistance to a particular interpretation as evidence that they are on the right track.

17. In anonymous surveys, Altemeyer found that 55 percent of his male students admitted they had used some form of force or manipulation in order to obtain sexual gratification from a woman; between 16 and 25 percent had either used physical force and/or alcohol or drugs to obtain intercourse (1996, 184). Results from Altemeyer's survey of female students corroborated the figures for men; 42 percent reported having been coerced or manipulated by a man, although women were more likely to say they had been forcibly raped than men were to admit to the crime (185).

18. *The Story of O* was a best seller and some are still inclined to consider it revolutionary. For instance, according to B. Creed (2003), "*The Story of O* attests to the transgressive power of the female novelist and artist" (69).

19. "It seems to me more and more that the essential point of hysteria is that it results from perversion on the part of the seducer, and more and more that heredity is seduction by the father," Freud (1985) wrote to Fliess on December 6, 1896. Hysteria was understood to be an experience of intense fear and panic, often expressed via the body as a specific disorder such as paralysis, stuttering, indigestion, etc. The goal of analytic treatment was to enable the patient to become conscious of the connection between the symptoms and the cause. According to the seduction theory, the cause was sexual abuse; Freud abandoned this idea in favor of a universal oedipal explanation in which girls desire to be "seduced" by their fathers.

20. Modern proponents of "false memory syndrome," a condition supposedly induced by therapists who persuade their patients to recall false memories of childhood sexual abuse, find much to criticize in Freud's clinical techniques. On this point at

least, they have reason to be concerned. In applying his theory clinically, Freud (1896) reported, "One only succeeds in awakening the psychical trace of a precocious sexual event under the most energetic pressure of the analytic procedure, and against an enormous resistance. Moreover, the memory must be extracted from them piece by piece" (153).

21. Years after he abandoned the seduction theory for oedipal ideas, Freud wrote, "You will recall an interesting episode in the history of analytic research which caused me many distressing hours. In the period in which the main interest was directed to discovering infantile sexual traumas, almost all my women patients told me that they had been seduced by their father. I was driven to recognise in the end that these reports were untrue and so came to understand that hysterical symptoms are derived from fantasies and not from real occurrences" (1933b, 120).

Chapter 3. Offensive Women

1. Age-of-consent laws for women in the United States range from sixteen to eighteen and are often modified by various provisions, such as whether the older party holds authority over the younger.

2. Golombok, Susan, et. al. 2003. "Children with Lesbian Parents: A Community Study." *Developmental Psychology* 39 (1): 20–33.

3. For instance, B. Mucklow and G. Phelan (1979) found that lesbians were as "nurturant" as heterosexual mothers. "Lesbian and Traditional Mothers' Responses to Child Behavior and Self-Concept." *Psychological Reports* 44: 880–82.

4. Although the historically significant Ohio trial (Hall vs. Hall) that featured Green's expert testimony dates to the mid-1970s, there continues to be a great deal of variation in what gay and lesbian parents can expect from the law and from judges when custody is in dispute. Currently in Ohio, as in more liberal states like California and Massachusetts, sexual orientation is not supposed to be taken into account unless there is evidence in a particular case that a parent's sexuality is having an adverse affect on her or his children's welfare. However, in many states, a gay or lesbian parent is still more likely to lose custody. The most famous case of the last decade, Bottoms vs. Bottoms, went to the Virginia Supreme Court, which denied the lesbian mother custody in part because "conduct inherent in lesbianism is punishable as a . . . felony" in Virginia, where sodomy laws still prohibit oral or anal sex in private between consenting adults (*Bottoms v. Bottoms*, 1995, 108).

5. A smattering of comments through the decades reveals the persistence of the idea that the big problems with women and their (often troubled) sexuality is that researchers haven't provided much data about them. "The result is . . . a relative lack of sufficient clinical experience in the psychiatric and psychoanalytic evaluation of female homosexuality"(E. Bergler 1948, 28); "Conspicuous neglect of the topic on the part of research workers, and a quite extraordinary dearth of factual information in published works, makes any statements about lesbianism peculiarly hazardous" (D. J. West 1967, 65); "Studies of groups of female homosexuals are largely lacking" (M. Saghir and E. Robins 1971, 503); "Lesbians present at clinics less frequently than do male homosexuals" (M. MacCullough and J. Waddington 1981, 341); "Few analysts, even of long ex-

perience have had the opportunity to treat more than a very small number of overtly homosexual women" (C. Socarides 1988, 184); "The dearth of genetic data on females is unfortunate" (J. M. Bailey et al. 1993, 217); and "Very little . . . research literature exists addressing the phenomenon of sexual abuse committed by *female* perpetrators" (A. Christiansen and B. Thyer 2002, 2).

6. Diana Russell (1999) has a comprehensive review of the literature on sexual abuse by females; her analysis is backed up by findings from a study of 930 women.

7. Among those who have cited Welldon are psychoanalysts, psychologists, and criminologists; they share the willingness to identify female perversions as maternal rather than, strictly speaking, sexual. See for instance A. Perkel (2004), A. Motz (2001), M. Denov (2001), M. Springer-Kremser et al. (2003), K. M. Beier (2000), D. Lloyd-Owen (2003), and M. Tardif et al. (2005).

8. "Pre-oedipal" refers to a time before reason, language, and the sense of one's self as an individual have asserted themselves in the developing child.

9. Although Burch maintained that heterosexual relationships are also likely to suffer from merger, "lesbian merger" is a focus of her work. This, as Burch recognized (1982), helps to sustain the conventional view that lesbians are particularly susceptible to losing self/other boundaries as a result of early problems with a mother-daughter bond.

10. For a collection of essays on the construction of Satanism, which the editors identify as a social problem without an objectively real foundation, see J. Best et al. (1991).

11. Later, Stoller would criticize what he came to consider the wholly inadequate system of classification. "This is a system?" he asked, and recommended starting over entirely (1985, 10–11).

12. Joyce McDougall (1979) used a similar idea to shore up views very different from Stoller's. She argued that women could not be true sexual partners for one another and that, therefore, the identity of a "female homosexual" is a fiction.

13. Although psychoanalysts have insisted on the immaturity of female homosexuality more vigorously than theorists in other disciplines, the theme found its way into more biologically based psychological models through the middle of the twentieth century. These models of female sexual development bear traces of an old idea that the male represents a higher order of evolutionary development than the female. According to Cynthia Russet's history of sexual science, an anatomist in 1821 observed that women "were less differentiated from the common, primitive, embryonic type" than men (74–75). In the 1880s, a zoologist discussing the relative maturity of the sexes stated that "when a female, from disease or mutilation or old age, assumes a resemblance to the male, the change is an advance," a claim that, had he considered the issue, would have required him to argue for the superiority of "masculine" female homosexuals relative to "feminine" heterosexual women (405).

14. Some of those who continue to believe in the efficacy of "reparative therapy" or other therapies to change sexual orientation include Spitzer, R. (2003) and Nicolosi, J. (2003). There is an organization, NARTH (National Association for Research and Therapy of Homosexuality), that represents practitioners of "reorientation therapy," which, like "reparative therapy," has the goal of making gay people heterosexual.

15. However, the government has identified other marginal groups, including African Americans and the poor, as salvageable. In 2006 the Bush administration decided to spend $100 million on programs to promote marriage.

Chapter 4. Theoretical Space

1. From 1990 to 2009, the MLA online index lists over a thousand journal articles in the humanities that use psychoanalytic theory. In the same period, PsychINFO, which indexes journals in every branch of psychology, lists over six thousand journal articles on psychoanalysis.

2. I use the terms *lesbian* and *lesbian development* throughout this chapter to indicate ideas of the lesbian as that figure is implicated in the construction of theory.

3. Freud never actually gave the lectures contained in *New Introductory Lectures on Psychoanalysis* publicly. The collection was a supplement to a series of lectures Freud delivered to university faculty at the Vienna Psychiatric Clinic in 1915–17. In *New Introductory Lectures,* Freud proposed to "take my place in the lecture room . . . by an artifice of the imagination" (5). His artificial audience was composed not of professional analysts, but of "the multitude of educated people to whom we may perhaps attribute a benevolent, even though cautious," interest in psychoanalysis (6).

4. Leslie Deutsch pointed out that women analysts who had been analyzed by Freud were most likely to produce theories that complemented his own (1995, 30).

5. See, for instance, C. Socarides (1988), J. McDougall (1979), and J. Quinodoz (1989).

6. American Psychoanalytic Association (1996). http://www.apsa-co.org/ctf/pubinfo/female.htm.

7. In her response to Rothenberg and Valente, Fuss argued that "staking out a 'pure' constructionist position reinscribes an essentialist logic, and that constructionists . . . need to be wary of acting as if essentialism had an essence" (384).

8. For an excellent discussion of women's responses to the Bobbitt case, both celebratory and condemning, see Linda Pershing (1996). Pershing reported that "during the Bobbitt trials, women came forward to announce that although they had never actually done so, they often wished they had found the courage to mutilate their own rapists" (19). Particularly pertinent to the issue of sexual difference was Lorena Bobbitt's dismay over her husband's financial extravagance; while she made $17,000 per year working six days a week, John Wayne Bobbitt lost job after job. Nevertheless, he continued to purchase luxuries she could not afford to give him, stealing from her to meet his expenses. For Lorena Bobbitt, these excesses seemed part and parcel of his sexual violence and abuse of her.

9. However, this is not to say that lesbian texts or visual media cannot engage successfully with psychoanalytic theory. Nicole Brossard's "These Our Mothers or: The Disintegrating Chapter" (1994), for instance, seemed to seek a dialogue with extant psychoanalytic strategies.

Conclusion

1. Butler was more concerned with the war over the term "gender," which the Vatican objected to on the ground that it was code for "homosexual" (181).

2. See, for instance, Elizabeth Freeman (2007) who finds herself "still embarrassingly here" after "queer theory has been pronounced over" (495). "Still After." *South Atlantic Quarterly* 106 (3): 495–500. On another view, queer theory will murder itself (or perhaps already has) by cleaving to "a vocabulary of melancholy, self-shattering, shame, and the death drive," according to Michael Snediker (2006), who recommends moving "beyond the futural" as a potential rescue strategy. "Queer Optimism." *Postmodern Culture* 16 (3): 2.

3. It explains, for instance, why "choice" is an impoverished and parochial notion in any of the following circumstances: if the activists who wield it fail to recognize that sterilization, contraception, adoption, infertility treatments, and abortion can all be used to oppress or liberate women; or if activists work only on behalf of women who are heterosexual, white, nontransgendered; or if they believe that "choice" can be exercised independent of one's culture; or if they believe that "choice" is a significant concept only when applied to reproduction.

4. Some features of the act will be familiar to critics of the U.S. policy on "enemy combatants," which allowed the government to arrest "anyone, anywhere in the world, label him an enemy combatant and hold him for as long as it wishes without any hearing or judicial review that might distinguish the innocent from the enemy" Cole, D. 2004. "Guantanamo Bay Continues as a Blot of Shame on the U.S." *Los Angeles Times*, February 22. http://www.latimes.com As I write, the people being held at Guantanamo are simply called "detainees."

5. Jeffreys, Sheila. 2004. "Allowing Alex's sex change shows up a gender-biased Family Court." *On Line Opinion: Australia's E-Journal of Social and Political Debate*, April 19.

6. Bravman, Scott. 1994. "The Lesbian and Gay Past: It's Greek to Whom?" *Gender, Place & Culture: A Journal of Feminist* Geography 1 (2): 149–70; and Brown, Michael, and Larry Knopp. 2008. "Queering the Map: The Productive Tensions of Colliding Epistemologies." *Annals of the Association of American Geographers* 98 (1): 40–58.

7. This works only with gender; if I try to do something similar with race, the results are unworkable. Even in queer theory, a white identity is stable in ways that a female or lesbian identity is not. A white person can allow her race to remain unmarked and unthought; she can modify it by asserting some cross-racial identity; or she can question its meaning, but she cannot exit her race through some process of transformation or disavowal.

8. See, for instance, Phyllis Chesler's *The Death of Feminism* (2005), in which the author tried to combine at attack on Western, non-Muslim feminists with an account of how bad Islamic fundamentalism is for women. As Carol Anne Douglas put it in her review of the book, if Chesler "believes Islamic fundamentalism really is the main threat to the world, why devote more words to criticizing Robin Morgan and Katha Pollitt . . . than to Osama bin Laden?" *off our backs* 36 (3): 56–60.

9. Mary Hawkesworth (2004) wrote a fascinating and comprehensive history of the interminable death of feminism, evoking the question of whether it is possible to kill feminism by repeatedly announcing its death: "With no corpse, no proof of demise, just vague hints of self-inflicted wounds and natural causes, feminism's death by report erases the social justice activism of women around the globe while covering the traces of the

erasure" (983). "The Semiotics of Premature Burial: Feminism in a Postfeminist Age." *Signs: Journal of Women in Culture and Society* 29 (4): 961–85.

10. My mother would not recognize her own mother-and-daughterhood in "womon-born womon." If I wished to apply the phrase to my own origins while respecting her self-naming, I would have to write "woman-born womon," but I cannot see that the difference between us is so great that I need a different vowel.

11. Camp Trans '99: The Pre-Event Buildup. http://www.camptrans.com/archive/1999 fdbk_ pre.html.

References

Allen, P. G. 1998. "Father God and Rape Culture." In *Off the Reservation: Reflections on Boundary-Busting, Border-Crossing Loose Canons.* Boston: Beacon.

Altemeyer, B. 1992. "Research Report: Authoritarianism, Religious Fundamentalism, Quest, and Prejudice." *International Journal for the Psychology of Religion* 2 (2): 113–33.

———. 1996. *The Authoritarian Specter.* Cambridge: Harvard University Press.

Althusser, L. 1992. *The Future Lasts Forever. A Memoir.* New York: New Press.

———. 1994. "Ideology and Ideological State Apparatuses." In *Mapping Ideology,* ed. Z. Slavoj, Verso. 100–140.

Bacon, C. L. 1965. "A Developmental Theory of Female Homosexuality." In *Perversions, Psychodynamics and Therapy,* ed. S. Lorand, 131–59. London: Ortolan.

Bailey, J., R. Pillar, M. Neale, and V. Agye. 1993. "Heritable Factors Influence Sexual Orientation in Women." *Archives of General Psychiatry* 50:217–23.

Bancroft, J. 1994. "Homosexual Orientation: The Search for a Biological Basis." *British Journal of Psychiatry* 164:437–40.

Barad, K. Summer 1998. "Getting Real: Technoscientific Practices and the Materialization of Reality." *difference: a journal of feminist cultural studies* 10:87–126.

Beier, K. M. 2000. "Female Analogies to Perversion." *Journal of Sex and Marital Therapy* 26 (1): 79–93.

Bergler, E. 1943. "The Respective Importance of Reality and Phantasy in the Genesis of Female Homosexuality." *Journal of Criminal Psychopathology* 5:27–48.

Best, J., D. Bromley, and J. Richardson, eds. 1991. *The Satanism Scare.* New York: Aldine de Gruyter.

Bikis, G. 1999. "Cleo's Back." In *Hers 3: Brilliant New Writing by Lesbian Writers,* ed. T. Wolverton and R. Drake, 39–56. New York: Faber and Faber.

Blyth, S., and G. Straker. 1996. "Intimacy, Fusion and Frequency of Sexual Contact in Lesbian Couples." *South African Journal of Psychology* 264:253–56.

Boas, F. 1940. *Race, Language, and Culture.* New York: Macmillan.

Bogaert, A. 1998. "Physical Development and Sexual Orientation in Women: Height, Weight, and Age of Puberty Comparisons." *Personality and Individual Differences* 24 (1): 115–21.

Bowditch, G. 2007. "Sex Missionary Under Fire." *Sunday Times,* January 14.

Braidotti, R. 1989. "The Politics of Ontological Difference." In *Between Feminism and Psychoanalysis*, ed. T. Brennan, 89–105. London: Routledge.

———. 1994. *Nomadic Subjects: Embodiment and Sexual Difference in Contemporary Feminist Theory.* New York: Columbia University Press.

———. 1997. "Comment on Felski's 'The Doxa of Difference': Working through Sexual Difference." *Signs: Journal of Women in Culture and Society* 231:23–40.

Brody, S. 2006. "Penile–Vaginal Intercourse is Better: Evidence Trumps Ideology." *Sexual and Relationship Therapy* 21 (4): 393–403.

Brontë, C. 1993. *Jane Eyre.* New York: Oxford University Press.

Brossard, N. 1994. "These Our Mothers or: The Disintegrating Chapter." In *The Penguin Book of Lesbian Short Stories*, ed. by M. Reynolds, 183–203. New York: Penguin Books.

Brown, W. M. 2002. "Differences in Finger Length Ratios between Self-Identified 'Butch' and 'Femme' Lesbians." *Archives Of Sexual Behavior* 311:123–27.

Bull, C. 2001. "Much Ado About Changing." *The Advocate* 840:30–32.

Burch, B. 1982. "Psychological Merger in Lesbian Couples: A Joint Ego Psychological and Systems Approach." *Family Therapy* 9 (3): 201–8.

———. 1993. "Heterosexuality, Bisexuality, and Lesbianism: Rethinking Psychoanalytic Views of Women's Sexual Object Choice." *Psychoanalytic Review* 80 (1): 83–99.

Butler, J. 1990. *Gender Trouble: Feminism and the Subversion of Identity.* New York: Routledge.

Card, C. 1995. *Lesbian Choices.* New York: Columbia University Press.

Carter, J. 1997. "Normality, Whiteness, Authorship: Evolutionary Sexology and the Primitive Pervert." In *Science and Homosexualities*, ed. V. A. Rosario, 155–76. New York: Routledge.

Chasseguet-Smirgel, J. 1991. "Sadomasochism in the Perversions: Some Thoughts on the Destruction of Reality." *Journal of the American Psychoanalytic Association* 39 (2): 399–415.

Chodorow, N. 1978. *The Reproduction of Mothering: Psychoanalysis and the Sociology of Gender.* Berkeley: University of California Press.

———. 1989. *Feminism and Psychoanalytic Theory.* New Haven: Yale University Press.

———. 1994. *Femininities, Masculinities, Sexualities: Freud and Beyond.* Lexington: University Press of Kentucky.

Christian, B. 1993. "Trajectories of Self–Definition: Placing Contemporary Afro–American Women's Fiction." In *Feminisms: an Anthology of Literary Theory and Criticism*, ed. R. Warhol and D. Hernd, 316–33. New Brunswick: Rutgers University Press.

Christiansen, A. and B. Thyer, 2002. "Female Sexual Offenders: A Review of Empirical Research." *Journal of Behavior in the Social Environment* 6 (3): 1–16.

Clarke, C. 1989. *Humid Pitch: Narrative Poetry.* Ithaca, NY: Firebrand Books.

———. 1993a. *Experimental Love.* Ithaca, NY: Firebrand Books.

———. 1993b. "Living the Texts Out: Lesbians and the Uses of Black Women's Traditions." In *Theorizing Black Feminisms: The Visionary Pragmatism of Black Women*, ed. S. James and A. Busia, 214–27. New York: Routledge.

Coleman, E., Gooren, L. and Ross, M. et. al. 1989. "Theories of Gender Transpositions: A Critique and Suggestions for Further Research." *Journal of Sex Research* 264:525–38.

Creed, B. 2003. *Media Matrix. Sexing the New Reality.* Crows Nest, NSW: Allen and Unwin.

Cvetkovich, A. 1995. "Sexual Trauma / Queer Memory: Incest, Lesbianism, and Therapeutic Culture." *GLQ: Journal of Lesbian and Gay Studies* 2:351–77.

Dancey, C. P. 1990. "Sexual Orientation in Women: An Investigation of Hormonal and Personality Variables." *Biological Psychology* 303:251–64.

de Lauretis, T. 1994. *The Practice of Love: Lesbian Sexuality and Perverse Desire.* Bloomington: Indiana University Press.

———. 1997. "Habit Changes. Response." In *Feminism Meets Queer Theory*, ed. E. Weed and N. Schor, 315–34. Bloomington: Indiana University Press.

D'Emilio, J. and E. Freedman. 1988. *Intimate Matters. A History of Sexuality in America.* New York: Harper and Row.

Denov, M. 2001. "A Culture of Denial: Exploring Professional Perspectives on Female Sex Offending." *Canadian Journal of Criminology* 43 (3): 303–29.

Desperately Seeking Susan. 1984. Prod. S. Pillsbury and M. Sanford. Dir. S. Seidelman. Orion Pictures.

Deutsch, L. 1995. "Out of the Closet and onto the Couch: A Psychoanalytic Exploration of Lesbian Development." In *Lesbians and Psychoanalysis: Revolutions in Theory and Practice*, ed. J. Glassgold and S. Iasenza, 19–38. New York: Free Press.

Dever, C. 1997. "Obstructive Behavior: Dykes in the Mainstream of Feminist Theory." In *Cross Purposes: Lesbians, Feminists, and the Limits of Alliance*, ed. D. Heller, 19–41. Bloomington: Indiana University Press.

Dickinson, R. L. and L. Beam. 1934. *The Single Woman: A Medical Study in Sex Education.* New York: Reynal & Hitchcock.

Dittmann, R. W., M. H. Kappes, M. E. Kappes, and D. Börger. 1992. "Sexual Behavior in Adolescent and Adult Females with Congenital Adrenal Hyperplasia." *Psychoneuroendocrinology.* 172–73. 153–70.

Dobson, J. 2001. "The State of the Family." *Focus on the Family.* family.org/docstudy/newsletters/A0016707.html.

Doell, R. 1995. "Sexuality in the Brain." *Journal of Homosexuality* 281:345–54.

Dörner, G. 1968. "Hormonal Induction and Prevention of Female Homosexuality." *Journal of Endocrinology* 42:163–64

Dörner, G. and J. Fatschel. 1970. "Effects of Neonatally Administered Androgens and Anti-Androgens on Sex Behavior and Fertility of Female Rats." *Endokrinologie* 561:29–48.

Dörner, G. and G. Hinz. 1972. "Neuroendocrine Predisposition for Female Homosexuality with Continuing Cyclic Function of the Ovary." *Endokrinologie* 591:48–52.

Dörner, G. F. Döcke, and S. Moustafa. 1968. "Homosexuality in Female Rats Following Testosterone Implantation in the Anterior Hypothalamus." *Journal Of Reproduction And Fertility* 171:173–75.

Douglas. M. 1966. *Purity and Danger: An Analysis of Concepts of Pollution and Taboo.* New York: Frederick A. Praeger.

Ehrhardt, A., et al. 1968. "Fetal Androgens and Female Gender Identity in the Early-Treated Adrenogenital Syndrome." *Johns Hopkins Medical Journal* 1223:160–67.

Ellis, H. 1897. *Sexual Inversion.* London: Wilson and MacMillan.

Ellis , L. and S. Cole-Harding. 2001. "The effects of prenatal stress, and of prenatal alcohol and nicotine exposure, on human sexual orientation. *Physiology and Behavior* 74:213–26.

Ensler, E. 1998. *The Vagina Monologues.* New York: Villard Books.

Fausto-Sterling, A. 1995. "Animal Models for the Development of Human Sexuality: A Critical Evaluation." *Journal of Homosexuality* 28 (3,4): 217–36.

Foucault, M. 1970. *The Order of Things.* New York: Pantheon Books.

———. 1978. *The History of Sexuality: Vol. I, An Introduction.* New York: Pantheon Books.

———. 1979. *Discipline and Punish: The Birth of the Prison.* Ed. A. Sheridan. New York: Vintage Books.

———. 1983. "The subject and power." In Michel Foucault, Beyond Structuralism and Hermeneutics, ed. H. Dreyfus and Rabinow, P. Chicago: University of Chicago Press, 1983.

Freud, S. 1896. "The Aetiology of Hysteria." In *The Standard Edition of the Complete Works of Sigmund Freud,* Ed. J. Strachey., 3:189–221. London: Hogarth.

———. 1917. "Paths to the Formation of Symptoms." In *The Complete Introductory Lectures on Psychoanalysis,* Ed. J. Strachey. New York: W. W. Norton.

———. 1927. *The Ego and the Id.* Translated by Joan Riviere. London: Hogarth Press.

———. 1933a. "My Contact with Josef Popper-Lynkeus." In *The Standard Edition of the Complete Works of Sigmund Freud,* ed. J. Strachey, 22:219–24. London: Hogarth.

———. 1933b. "Psychogenesis of a Case of Female Homosexuality." In vol. 5, *Collected Papers.* London: Hogarth.

———. 1961. *Civilization and its Discontents.* Trans. J. Strachey. New York: W. W. Norton.

———. 1964. *The Future of an Illusion.* Trans. W. Robson-Scott, ed. J. Strachey. New York: Anchor Books.

———. 1985. *The Complete Letters of Sigmund Freud to Wilhelm Fliess, 1887–1904.* ed. J. M. Masson. Cambridge: Harvard University Press.

Fuss, D. 1992. "Fashion and the Homospectatorial Look." *Critical Inquiry* 18 (4): 713–37.

———. 1996. "Look Who's Talking, or if Looks Could Kill." *Critical Inquiry* 22 (2): 383–93.

Garrett-Gooding, J. and R. Senter. 1987. "Attitudes and Acts of Sexual Aggression on a University Campus." *Sociological Inquiry* 59:348–71.

Gartrell, N. 1981. "The Lesbian as a 'Single' Woman." *American Journal of Psychotherapy* 35 (4): 502–16.

Gartrell, N., and Banks, A. et al. 1977a. "Hormones and Sexual Orientation. A Questionable Link." *Journal of Homosexuality* 283 (4): 247–68.

Gartrell, N., et al. 1977b. "Plasma Testosterone in Homosexual and Heterosexual Women." *American Journal of Psychiatry* 13410:1117–19.

Gibson, M. 1997. "Clitoral Corruption: Body Metaphors and American Doctors' Constructions of Female Homosexuality, 1870–1900." In *Science and Homosexualities*, Ed. V. Rosario, 108–32. New York: Routledge.

Green, R. 1992. *Sexual Science and the Law*. Cambridge: Harvard University Press.

Greendlinger, V., and D. Byrne. 1987. "Coercive Sexual Fantasies of College Men as Predictors of Self-Reported Likelihood to Rape and Overt Sexual Aggression." *The Journal of Sex Research* 23:1–11.

Griggers, C. 1992. "Lesbian Bodies In The Age Of PostMechanical Reproduction." *Postmodern Culture* 2 (3): 15.

Grosz, E. 1997. "The Labors of Love: Analyzing Perverse Desire: An Interrogation of Teresa de Lauretis's *The Practice Of Love*." In *Feminism Meets Queer Theory*, ed. E. Weed and N. Schor, 293–314. Bloomington: Indiana University Press.

Halberstam, J. 1998. *Female Masculinity*. Durham: Duke University Press.

Halliday, C. 1990. "The 'Naked Majesty of God': Contemporary Lesbian Erotic Poetry." In *Lesbian and Gay Writing: An Anthology of Critical Essays*, ed. M. Lilly. Philadelphia: Temple University Press.

Halperin, D. 1993. "Is There a History of Sexuality?" In *The Lesbian and Gay Studies Reader*, ed. H. Abelove, M. Barale, and D. Halperin. 416–431. New York: Routledge.

Halpern, D. F. 2000. *Sex Differences in Cognitive Abilities*. Mahwah NJ: Lawrence Erlbaum Associates.

Hammonds, E. 1997. "Black Wholes and the Geometry of Black Female Sexuality." In *Feminism Meets Queer Theory*, ed. E. Weed and N. Schor, 136–56. Bloomington: Indiana University Press.

Haraway, D. 1997. *Modest_Witness@Second_Millennium. FemaleMan©_Meets _Onco mouse™*. New York: Routledge.

Henry, G. 1941. *Sex Variants. A Study of Homosexual Patterns*. New York: Paul B. Hoeber.

Hobbes, T. 1904. *Leviathan, or the Matter, Forme, and Power of a Common-Wealth Ecclesiasticall, and Civil*. Ed. A. R. Waller. Cambridge, MA: Cambridge University Press.

Hodges, A. 1983. *Alan Turing: The Enigma*. New York: Simon and Schuster.

Hrdy, S. 1996. "The Evolution of Female Orgasms: Logic Please but no Atavism." *Animal Behaviour* 52:851–52.

Hughes, M. 1997. "Personal Experiences-Professional Interests: Joan Riviere and Femininity." *International Journal of Psycho-Analysis* 78 (5): 899–911.

James, W. 2005. "Biological and Psychosocial Determinants of Male and Female Human Sexual Orientation." *Journal of Biosocial Science* 375:555–67.

Jeffreys, S. 2003. *Unpacking Queer Politics: A Lesbian Feminist Perspective*. Oxford: Blackwell, 2003.

Jiménez, J. 2004. "A Psychoanalytical Phenomenology of Perversion." *International Journal of Psychoanalysis* 85 (1): 65–82.

Jordan, K. M., and R. H. Deluty. 1995. “Clinical Interventions by Psychologists with Lesbians and Gay Men.” *Journal of Clinical Psychology* 513:448–56.

Jureidini, J. 2001. “Perversion: Erotic Form of Hatred Or Exciting Avoidance Of Reality?” *Journal of the American Academy of Psychoanalysis and Dynamic Psychiatry* 29 (2): 195–211.

Kaufman, P. A., E. Harrison, and M. Hyde. 1984. “Distancing for Intimacy in Lesbian Relationships.” *American Journal of Psychiatry* 1414:530–33.

Kenyon, F. E. 1968a. “Physique and Physical Health of Female Homosexuals.” *Journal of Neurology. Neurosurgery and Psychiatry* 315:487–89.

———. 1968b. “Sexual Development: Attitudes and Experience.” *British Journal of Psychiatry* 114 (516): 1343–50.

Kirsch, M. 2000. *Queer Theory and Social Change*. New York: Routledge.

Kishner, L. 2003. “The Man Who Didn’t Exist.” *American Imago* 60 (2): 211–39.

Koedt, A. 1973. “The Myth of the Vaginal Orgasm.” In *Radical Feminism*, ed. A. Koedt, E. Levine, and A. Rapune. New York: Quadrangle Books.

Koss, M., and C. Oros. 1982. “Sexual Experiences Survey: A Research Instrument Investigating Sexual Aggression and Victimization.” *Journal of Consulting and Clinical Psychology* 50:455–57.

Krestan, J., and C. Bepko. 1980. “The Problem of Fusion in the Lesbian Relationship.” *Family Process* 19:277–89.

Laqueur, T. 1987. *The Making of the Modern Body: Sexuality and Society in the Nineteenth Century*. Berkeley: University of California Press.

Lasch, C. 1981. “The Freudian Left and the Theory of Cultural Revolution.” *Dimensions of Psychoanalysis*, ed. J. Sandler and J. Bowlby, 123–38. Madison, CT: International Universities Press.

Latour, B. 1994. “Pragmatogonies: A Mythical Account of How Humans and Nonhumans Swap Properties.” *American Behavioral Scientist* 37 (6): 791–808.

Latour, B., and S. Woolgar. 1986. *Laboratory Life. The Construction of Scientific Facts*. Princeton: Princeton University Press.

LeVay, S. 1996. *Queer Science: The Uses and Abuses of Research into Homosexuality*. Cambridge: MIT Press.

LeVay, S. 1993. “We Can Get There from Here: Ideals and Strategies.” *Nation* 257:26–31.

Lev-Ran, A. 1974. “Sexuality and Educational Levels of Women with Late-Treated Andrenogenital Syndrome.” *Archives of Sexual Behavior* 31:27–32.

Lindenbaum, J. 1985. “The Shattering of an Illusion. The Problem of Competition in Lesbian Relationships.” *Feminist Studies* 111:85–103.

Lippa, R. A. 2003. “Are 2D.4D Finger-Length Ratios Related to Sexual Orientation? Yes for Men, No for Women.” *Journal of Personality and Social Psychology* 85 (1): 179–88.

Lloyd-Owen, D. 2003. “Perverse Females: Their Unique Psychopathology.” *British Journal of Psychotherapy* 19 (3): 285–96.

Loehlin, J., and D. McFadden. 2003. “Comparison of the Auditory Systems of Heterosexuals and Homosexuals: Click-Evoked Otoacoustic Emissions.” *Archives of Sexual Behavior* 322:115–27.

Lorde, A. 1993. *Zami: A New Spelling of My Name.* New York: Triangle Classics.

MacCullough, M., and J. Waddington. 1981. "Neuroendocrine Mechanism and the Aetiology of Male and Female Homosexuality." *British Journal of Psychiatry* 139:341–45.

Malamuth, N. M., R. Sockloskie, M. Koss, and J. Tanaka. 1991. "Characteristics of Aggressors against Women: Testing a Model Using a National Sample of College Students." *Journal of Consulting and Clinical Psychology* 59:670–81.

Martin, E. 1996. "The Egg and Sperm: How Science had Constructed a Romance Based on Stereotypical Male-Female Roles." In *Feminism and Science,* ed. E. Keller and H. Longino, 103–20. New York: Oxford University Press.

Masters, W., and V. Johnson. 1966. *Human Sexual Response.* Boston: Little, Brown.

Matthews, J., Matthews, R. and Speltz, K. et al. 1991. "Female Sexual Offenders: A Typology." In *Family Sexual Abuse: Frontline Research and Evaluation,* ed. M. Patton, 199–219. Newbury Park, CA: Sage Publications.

Mbügua, K. 2006. "Reasons to Suggest that the Endocrine Research on Sexual Preference is a Degenerating Research Program." *History and Philosophy of the Life Sciences* 28 (3): 337–58.

McDougall, J. 1979. "The Homosexual Dilemma." In *Sexual Deviations,* ed. I. Rosen, 206–45. Oxford: Oxford University Press.

McFadden, D. 2003. "The Relationships between Otoacoustic Emissions and Relative Lengths of Fingers and Toes in Humans." *Hormones and Behavior* 43 (3): 421–29.

McFadden, D., and E. G. Pasanen. 1998. "Comparison of the Auditory Systems of Heterosexuals and Homosexuals: Click-Evoked Otoacoustic Emissions." *Proceedings of the National Academy of Sciences of the United States* 955:2709–13.

———. 1999. "Spontaneous Otoacoustic Emissions in Heterosexuals, Homosexuals, and Bisexuals." *Journal of the Acoustical Society of America* 1054:2403–13.

Meyer, S. 1999. "Colonialism and the Figurative Strategy of Jane Eyre." In *Post-Colonial Theory and English Literature,* ed. P. Childs, 149–63. Edinburgh: Edinburgh University Press.

Miller, G. 1998. "A Review of Sexual Selection and Human Evolution: How Mate Choice Shaped Human Nature." In *Handbook of Evolution and Human Behavior: Ideas, Issues, and Applications,* ed. C. Crawford and D. Krebs, 87–130. Mahwah, NJ: Lawrence Erlbaum Associates.

Money, J. 1987. "Sin, Sickness, or Status? Homosexual Gender Identity and Psychoneuroendocrinology." *American Psychologist* 424:384–99.

Money, J., and V. Lewis. 1987. "Bisexually Concordant, Heterosexually And Homosexually Discordant: A Matched-Pair Comparison of Male and Female Adrenogenital Syndrome." *Psychiatry. Journal for the Study of Interpersonal Processes* 502:97–111.

Morris, J., K. Gobrogge, C. Jordan and S. M. Breedlove. 2004. "Brain Aromatase: Dyed-in-the-Wool Homosexuality." *Endocrinology* 145 (2): 475–77.

Motz, A. 2001. *The Psychology of Female Violence. Crimes against the Body.* New York: Brunner-Routledge.

Müller, M., F. Bidlingmaier, C. förster, and D. Knorr. 1982. "Psychosexual Behavior of Females with Adrenogenital Syndrome." *Helvetica Paediatrica Acta* 376:571–80.

Nathan, P., and T. Ward. 2002. "Female Sex Offenders: Clinical and Demographic Features." *Journal of Sexual Aggression* 8 (1): 5–21.

Nicolosi, J. 2003. "Finally, Recognition of a Long-Neglected Population." *Archives of Sexual Behavior* 32:445–47.

Nisbet, R. 1970. *The Social Bond.* New York: Alfred A. Knopf.

O'Connor, N., and J. Ryan. 1993. *Wild Desires & Mistaken Identities: Lesbianism and Psychoanalysis.* New York: Columbia University Press.

Osland, J. A., Fitch, M., and Willis, E. et al. 1996. "Likelihood to Rape in College Males." *Sex Roles: A Journal of Research* 35 (3,4): 171–83.

Pardie, L., and C. Herb. 1997. "Merger and Fusion in Lesbian Relationships: A Problem of Diagnosing What's Wrong in Terms of What's Right." *Women and Therapy* 20 (3): 51–61.

Pateman, C. 1980. *The Disorder of Women: Democracy, Feminism, and Political Theory.* Stanford, CA: Stanford University Press.

———. 1988. *The Sexual Contract.* Stanford: Stanford University Press.

Pearcey, S. M., K. Docherty and J. Dabbs. 1996. "Testosterone and Sex Role Identification in Lesbian Couples." *Physiology and Behavior* 603:1033–35.

Pearlman, S. 1988. "Distancing and Connectedness: Impact on Couple Formation in Lesbian Relationships." *Women and Therapy* 81:77–88.

Perkel, A. 2004. "The First Seduction: Exploring Resistance to the Acknowledgement of Maternal Sexual Abuse." *Psycho-Analytic Psychotherapy in South Africa* 12 (2): 52–71.

Perkins, M. 1981. "Female Homosexuality and Body Build." *Archives of Sexual Behavior* 10 (4): 337–45.

Perloff, W. 1949. "Hormones in Human Sexuality." *Psychosomatic Medicine* 113:133–39.

Peterson, S. A., and B. Franzese, 1987. "Correlates of College Men's Sexual Abuse of Women." *Journal of College Student Personnel* 28:223–28.

Phillips, A. 1992. "Universal Pretensions in Political Thought." In *Destabilizing Theory: Contemporary Feminist Debates,* ed. M. Barrett and A. Phillips, 10–30. Stanford, CA: Stanford University Press.

Prince, M. 1898. "Sexual Perversion or Vice? A Pathological and Therapeutic Inquiry," *Journal of Nervous and Mental Disease* 25:237–56. Repr. *Psychotherapy and Multiple Personality: Selected Essays,* ed. Nathan G. Hale. Cambridge, MA: Harvard University Press, 1975.

Rahman, Q. 2005. "Fluctuating Asymmetry: Second to Fourth Finger Length Ratios and Human Sexual Orientation." *Psychoneuroendocrinology* 30 (4): 382–91.

Randall, M. 1987. *This is about Incest.* Ithaca, NY: Firebrand Books.

Rapaport, K., and B. R. Burkhart. 1984. "Personality and Attitudinal Characteristics of Sexually Coercive College Males." *Journal of Abnormal Psychology* 93:216–22.

Ricketts, W. 1984. "Biological Research on Homosexuality: Ansell's Cow or Occam's Razor?" *Journal of Homosexuality* 94:65–93.

Riviere, J. 1929. "Womanliness as a Masquerade." *International Journal of Psycho-Analysis* 10:303–13.

Rose, J. 1989. "Where Does the Misery Come From? Psychoanalysis, Feminism, and the Event." In *Feminism and Psychoanalysis*, ed. R. Feldstein and J. Roof, 25–39. Ithaca: Cornell University Press.

Rothenberg, M., and R. Valente, 1996. "Fashionable Theory and Fashion–Able Women: Returning Fuss's Homospectatorial Look." *Critical Inquiry* 22 (2): 372–82.

Rousseau, J. 1994. *Discourse on Political Economy and the Social Contract*. Trans. C. Betts. Oxford: Oxford University Press.

Rubin, G. 1999. "Thinking Sex: Notes for a Radical Theory of the Politics of Sexuality." *Culture, Society and Sexuality: A Reader,* ed. P. Parker, 143–78. London: UCL Press.

Rucker, N., and K. L. Lombardi. 1990. "The Familial Menage-à-Trois: Mother-Daughter Sexuality and Father-Daughter Incest." *Journal of Contemporary Psychotherapy* 20 (2): 99–107.

Russell, D. 1999. *The Secret Trauma: Incest in the Lives of Girls and Women*. New York: Basic Books.

Russet, C. 1989. *Sexual Science: The Victorian Construction of Womanhood*. Cambridge: Harvard University Press.

Saghir, M., and E. Robins. 1971. "Male and Female Homosexuality: Natural History." *Comprehensive Psychiatry* 126:503–10.

Sherfey, M. J. 1966. *Nature and Evolution of Female Sexuality*. New York: Random House.

Siegal, T. 1993. "Female To Male." *Off Our Backs* 23 (9): 4.

Singh, D., M. Vidaurri, R. Zambarano, and J. Dabbs. 1999. "Lesbian Erotic Role Identification: Behavioral, Morphological and Hormonal Correlates." *Journal of Personality and Social Psychology* 766:1035–49.

Socarides, C. 1970. "Homosexuality and Medicine." *JAMA* 72 (12): 1199–1202.

———. 1978. *Homosexuality*. New York: J. Aronson.

———. 1988. *The Preoedipal Origin and Psychoanalytic Therapy of Sexual Perversions*. Madison, WI: International Universities Press.

Somerville, S. 1994. "Scientific Racism and the Emergence of the Homosexual Body." *Journal of the History of Sexuality* 5:243–66.

Spitzer, R. 2001. "Commentary: Psychiatry and Homosexuality." *Wall Street Journal*, May 23.

———. 2003. "Can Some Gay Men and Lesbians Change Their Sexual Orientation? 200 Participants Reporting a Change from Homosexual to Heterosexual Orientation." *Archives of Sexual Behavior* 32:403–17.

Springer-Kremser, M., K. Leithner, M. Fischer, and H. Löffler-Stast Ka. 2003. "Gender and Perversion—What Constitutes a 'Bad Mother.'" *Archives of Women's Mental Health* 6 (2): 109–14.

Stacey, J. 1987. "Desperately Seeking Difference." *Screen* 28 (1): 48–61.

Stelboum, J. 2001. "Editor's Introduction." *Harrington Lesbian Fiction Quarterly* 2 (1): 1–2.

Stevens, P. E., and J. M. Hall. 1988. "Stigma: Health Beliefs and Experiences with Health Care in Lesbian Women." *Image. Journal of Nursing Scholarship* 20:69–73.

Stoller, R. 1975. *Perversion: The Erotic Form of Hatred.* New York: Pantheon Books.

———. 1985. *Observing the Erotic Imagination.* New Haven: Yale University Press.

Sullivan, A. 2000. "The He Hormone." *New York Times Magazine,* April 2.

Tardif, M., N. Auclair, M. Jacob, and J. Carpenter. 2005. "Sexual Abuse Perpetrated by Adult and Juvenile Females: An Ultimate Attempt to Resolve a Conflict Associated with Maternal Identity." *Child Abuse and Neglect* 29 (2): 153–67.

Terry, J. 1999. *An American Obsession: Science, Medicine, and Homosexuality in Modern Society* Chicago: University of Chicago Press.

Tiefer, L. 1995. *Sex is Not a Natural Act.* Boulder, CO: Westview.

Tieger, T. 1981. "Self-Rated Likelihood of Raping and the Social Perception of Rape." *Journal of Research in Personality* 15:147–58.

Traub, V. 1995. "The Psychomorphology of the Clitoris." *GLQ: Journal of Lesbian and Gay Studies* 2:301–29.

Walters, S. D. 1996. "From Here to Queer: Radical Feminism, Postmodernism, and the Lesbian Menace or, Why Can't a Woman be More Like a Fag?" *Signs: A Journal of Women in Culture and Society* 21:830–69.

Welldon, E. 1988. *Mother, Madonna, Whore: The Idealization and Denigration Of Women.* New York: Guilford.

West, D. J. 1967. *Homosexuality.* London: Gerald Duckworth.

Williams, T., 2000. "Finger-Length Patterns and Sexual Orientation." *Nature* 404 (6777): 455–56.

Woolf, V. 1957. *A Room of One's Own.* New York: Harcourt Brace Jovanovich.

Wright, J. 2002. "Going Against the Grain: Hobbes's Case for Original Maternal Dominion." *Journal of Women's History* 14 (1): 123–27.

Index